W9-AAG-680

Praise for

THE PATH WITH HEART

by
Michael Lynberg

"One of those extraordinarily rare books—that is to say, if you want a gift to leave your children, give this one."
—M. Scott Peck, M.D.
Author of *The Road Less Traveled*

"*The Path with Heart* is a remarkable philosophical statement, reflecting not only sustained, careful thought on human values, but an impressive knowledge of the junction where science, philosophy and religion meet in the modern world. I admire not just the quality of the author's thought but the quality of his writing."
—Norman Cousins

"*The Path with Heart* is an enjoyable and enlightening book. I would be pleased to hear that it reaches many readers and that it has a salutary impact on those it does reach."

—Rabbi Harold Kushner
Author of *When Bad Things Happen to Good People*

Also by Michael Lynberg

THE PATH
WITH HEART

THE GIFT
OF GIVING

Michael Lynberg

Fawcett Columbine New York

Sale of this book without a front cover may be unauthorized. If this book is coverless, it may have been reported to the publisher as "unsold or destroyed" and neither the author nor the publisher may have received payment for it.

A Fawcett Columbine Book
Published by Ballantine Books
Copyright © 1991 by Michael Lynberg

All rights reserved under International and Pan-American Copyright Conventions. Published in the United States by Ballantine Books, a division of Random House, Inc., New York, and simultaneously in Canada by Random House of Canada Limited, Toronto.

Grateful acknowledgment is made to Henry Holt and Company, Inc. for permission to reprint an excerpt from *The Poetry of Robert Frost* edited by Edward Connery Lathem. Copyright 1916, © 1969 by Holt, Rinehart and Winston. Copyright 1944 by Robert Frost. Reprinted by permission of Henry Holt and Company, Inc.

Library of Congress Catalog Card Number: 91-70539
ISBN: 0-449-90615-9

Design by Holly Johnson

Manufactured in the United States of America

First Edition: October 1991
10 9 8 7 6 5 4 3 2 1

For my brother Doug
and my sister Julie

THE GIFT
OF GIVING

I

THE PARABLE OF

THE TALENTS

––––––

There is a story in the Bible, told by Jesus, in which a man is about to leave home on a trip. Before departing, he calls his servants and entrusts his property to them. He gives to each according to his ability: to one he gives five talents (a talent, at the time, being a measure of silver or currency), to the second he gives two talents, and to the third, one talent. Then he sets out on his journey.

The servant who receives five talents promptly goes and trades with them and makes five more. The man who receives two talents makes two more in the same way. But the man who receives one talent goes off and digs a hole in the ground and hides what his master has given him.

Sometime later, the master of these servants returns and goes through his accounts with them. The man who received five talents comes forward bringing

*I learned at least this by my experiments.
That if one advances confidently in the
direction of his dreams and endeavors
to live the life which he has imagined, he
will meet with a success unexpected
in common hours.*

HENRY DAVID THOREAU

God loves the world through us.

MOTHER TERESA

five more. "Sir," he says, "you entrusted me with five talents; here are five more that I have made." "Well done," says the master. "You have shown that you are trustworthy in handling small things, so now I will trust you with greater. Come and share in my happiness." Next, the servant who was given two talents comes forward. "Sir," he says, "you entrusted me with two talents; here are two more that I have made." The master is pleased: "Well done, good servant. You have shown yourself trustworthy in small things, now I will trust you with greater. Come and share in my happiness." Last comes forward the man who was given the single talent. "Sir," he says, "I had heard that you are a hard man, and I was afraid. So I went off and hid your talent in the ground. Look. Here it is. It was yours, now you can have it back." But his master answers him, "You wicked and lazy servant! So you knew that I was a hard man? Well then, you should have at least used your talent to earn interest. So now, take the talent away from him and give it to one who has ten talents. For to everyone who has, more will be given, and he will have more than enough. But the person who has not will be deprived even of what he has. As for this useless servant, throw him outside into the darkness!"

Like many stories in the Bible, the Parable of the Talents holds important truths on how we can best live our lives, on what we can do to make our existence most meaningful and fulfilling. Most biblical scholars interpret it as saying that God, like the master in the story, has given us each certain unique talents and abilities (the

Two roads diverged in a wood, and I—
I took the one less traveled by,
And that has made all the difference.
ROBERT FROST

This above all: to thine own self be true,
And it must follow, as the night the day,
Thou canst not be false to any man.
WILLIAM SHAKESPEARE

word *talent*, as we use it today, has its origin in this story). To live well, we must make use of these special abilities; in fact, we not only must use them, but we should go forth and try to multiply them, to make them grow. How much or what kind of talents we are given is not important; like the servants in the parable, we are each given different talents and in different measure. What is important is that we use them and expand upon them. Hiding from our talents, being lazy or burying them in fear under a pile of other concerns, is a sin against God and against life. It is better to try and lose than not to try at all.

There is indeed something special and unique about us all. Each person born into this world represents a force, an energy, a promise that has never occurred before and that will never occur again. Only one being like you, with your blend of characteristics and potentialities, will exist in eternity. Only one being like you, with your dreams and aspirations, with your wisdom and experience, born sometimes of joy but often of sorrow and pain, can ever be. In this lies a profound and challenging realization. If you do not live your life completely, realizing values and goals that you hold to be worthwhile, making your unique contribution to the world in which you live, nobody ever will. Your song will die with you.

The moments of your life, fleeting and irreplaceable, are opportunities to experience the wonders of existence, to "live deep and suck out all the marrow of life," as Thoreau endeavored to do. These opportunities

*Do not act as if you had
a thousand years to live.*
MARCUS AURELIUS

*The right man is the one
that seizes the moment.*
JOHANN WOLFGANG VON GOETHE

*Begin at once to live, and count
each day as a separate life.*
SENECA

are taken or lost forever. Likewise, the moments of your life are opportunities to use and build upon your special talents and abilities, to do the best you can, with what you have, where you are, and thus to give something back, in gratitude and in faith, for the gift of living.

Each of us has a certain style or spirit which we can bring to whatever tasks and responsibilities lie before us, ennobling the place where we stand by expressing what is highest in our nature. In this way, any work or activity that we do, from sweeping the floor to mending a fence, from caring for our children to helping a stranger in need, is challenging and significant, and can make use of our unique blend of talents and abilities. Wherever we are, whatever we do, we can strive to do it well, to express our vision of excellence, thereby expanding our talents and making our part of the world more truthful, beautiful, and caring. Our daily tasks and responsibilities may seem petty and insignificant, but they are the small brush strokes which together form a living canvas, with all the rich colors and compelling textures, that ultimately will make our lives a masterpiece.

Some of us are not sure what we want to do with our lives. Perhaps we feel that we do not have any talents worth developing; perhaps, in comparison with others, we feel ourselves to be inferior or inadequately prepared. But everybody has something to give, if only in kindness to one other living being, if only in reverence to one cubic inch of creation. In this lies the way to a life of greater meaning and purpose, to discovering and developing what is best in ourselves. "Everybody

*Do not lose heart, even if you must wait
a bit before finding the right thing, even if
you must make several attempts. Be
prepared for disappointments also! But do
not abandon your quest for the avocation,
for that sideline in which you can act
as a man for other men.*

ALBERT SCHWEITZER

*I know of no more encouraging fact
than the unquestionable ability of
man to elevate his life by
conscious endeavor.*

HENRY DAVID THOREAU

can be great," said Martin Luther King, Jr., "because anybody can serve. You don't have to have a college degree to serve. You don't have to make your subject and your verb agree to serve. You don't have to know about Plato and Aristotle to serve. You don't have to know about Einstein's theory of relativity to serve. You don't have to know the second theory of thermodynamics in physics to serve. You only need a heart full of grace. A soul generated by love."

It is in fulfilling the work before us, in striving for excellence in everything we do, that we come to discover ourselves and our true abilities. Self-knowledge, awareness of our unique gifts and potentialities, does not come solely from introspection, from thinking about what we are meant to do in life, but from testing ourselves against the world in which we live. "How can we learn to know ourselves?" asked Goethe. "Never by reflection, but by action. Try to do your duty and you will soon find out what you are. But what is your duty? The demands of the day." It is best, even if we are not sure what we want to do with our lives, to stay active, to make the most of the opportunities that we have at this time. In this way, our talents will reveal themselves. Furthermore, in fulfilling the work before us, we will grow in our capacity to do more. "The reward for doing one duty is the power to do another," says the Jewish Talmud.

Many of us, however, have already discovered what we want to do with our lives. We have a vision, a purpose that resonates to the very core of our being. Somehow we know that our lives will never be complete

Work is the inevitable condition of human life, the true source of human welfare.

LEO TOLSTOY

Blessed is he who has found his work; let him ask no other blessedness, he has a life-purpose; he has found it and will follow it.

THOMAS CARLYLE

unless we answer this calling. A part of us, that part which is most precious and unique, will always remain unfulfilled unless we find the courage and determination to step out from the crowd and be different, to live up to the standards of our heart rather than to the expectations of those around us.

Some of us, for example, are blessed with a special dream or vision, a cherished idea, that we feel compelled to bring forth from our imagination and into reality so that it may be of benefit to our fellowman. Perhaps we have a talent for invention and have thought of a certain product or service, or the improvement of an existing one, that could bring comfort or joy into the lives of others; perhaps we have thought of a way to alleviate some of the world's terrible suffering. "Some men see things as they are and say why?" said the poet Robert Frost. "I dream of things that never were and say why not?" Giving birth to your idea, feeding and caring for it, carefully dressing it and bringing it into the world, loving it even when it sometimes rejects your best efforts, may be the expression of your highest talents.

Others among us are gifted with a certain skill or ability, for teaching, for example, or for medicine, nursing, or scientific research, at which we may truly excel and make a contribution. To make use of our talents, to follow our heart in this direction, we may have to forgo an easier, more immediately rewarding path and go through many years of difficult study and rigorous training. Perhaps our research will take us to the far reaches of the globe or keep us many nights in the world

To business that we love we rise betime,
And go to't with delight.
WILLIAM SHAKESPEARE

Only he is successful in his business
who makes that pursuit which affords
him the highest pleasure sustain him.
HENRY DAVID THOREAU

The man who is born with a talent
which he is meant to use, finds his
greatest happiness in using it.
JOHANN WOLFGANG VON GOETHE

of our laboratory; perhaps our desire to help others will lead us away from comfort and security and into the hard world of the poor and the destitute. But this, or something like it, may be what calls out our highest talents, enabling us to live our lives most fully.

Many of us may feel that our talents and abilities call us to be a part of a business or organization in which we can work with others toward some common, worthwhile goal. Perhaps we have an interest in computers, for example, or in broadcasting, publishing, aviation, or public service. Maybe our talents are highly specialized or lie in coordinating, marketing, or selling the products and services of others. There are many things which require the concerted efforts of a number of individuals, striving together toward some common goal, each fulfilling his unique capabilities. In working together, we are able to accomplish more than any could accomplish alone; in harmony with others, our song may become an elegant concerto or a powerful symphony.

Some of us are called to more vigorous and physical pursuits, combining the love in our hearts with the strength in our arms to cultivate the earth, to harvest grain, or to fashion this grain into the bread that we eat. We may like to build things, to blend intelligence with skill to create homes, roads, bridges, ships, hospitals, universities—any of the thousands of things that make our lives safer, more comfortable and enriching. Or maybe we like to fix and repair what has already been built, believing that it is good to conserve and make last,

*Once I asked my confessor for advice
about my vocation. I asked, "How can I
know if God is calling me and for what
He is calling me?" He answered,
"You will know by your happiness. If you
are happy with the idea that God calls you
to serve Him and your neighbor, this will
be the proof of your vocation. Profound
joy of the heart is like a magnet that
indicates the path of life. One has to
follow it, even though one enters
into a way full of difficulties."*

MOTHER TERESA

rather than to throw away, which has become so tragically easy and prevalent in our world.

Then there are those drawn to the arts, who are, as Aleksandr Solzhenitsyn remarked in his Nobel Prize address, "given to sense more keenly than others the harmony of the world and all the beauty and savagery of man's contribution to it—and to communicate this poignantly to people." In your heart you may wish to be a painter, an actor, a writer, or a musician. You may be willing to give your life for your art, to sacrifice everything for creative excellence, beauty, and truth. This sacrifice may be necessary, for the life of the artist, while full of adventure and the thrill of creativity and discovery, can also be lonely and without the rewards valued by much of society. "Perhaps it will turn out that you are called to be an artist," wrote Ranier Maria Rilke in his *Letters to a Young Poet*. "Then take that destiny upon yourself and bear it, its burden and its greatness, without asking what recompense might come from the outside. For the creator must be a world for himself." And Carl Jung observed that it is sometimes necessary for the artist, in developing his talents and giving expression to his art, "to sacrifice happiness and everything that makes life worth living for the ordinary human being."

No matter where we are in life, whether we are doing our best to provide for a family and to fulfill the responsibilities before us, or whether we have the freedom and inclination to pursue our life's dream, all of us have a special quality or talent, a special vision or ability, that must be discovered and developed, that must be

*Many persons have a wrong idea of
what constitutes true happiness. It is
not attained through self-gratification,
but through fidelity to a worthy purpose.*

HELEN KELLER

*The secret of being miserable is to have
leisure to bother about whether you
are happy or not. The cure for it
is occupation.*

GEORGE BERNARD SHAW

explored and expressed, if we are to live our lives fully. This will draw our deepest love, make use of our greatest powers, and become our most valuable gift to the world in which we live.

Unfortunately, many of us remain a stranger to what is highest and most noble in our nature. Sometimes this is not our fault; we would like to move forward, but we have been injured by the harshness of life, and we are, for the moment at least, unable to answer our calling. Perhaps we have lost something of value—a loved one, our health, a dream, or an ideal—and there is a dark emptiness, a bewildering vacuum, that we are struggling to understand and fill. Or perhaps our hearts were wounded by betrayal; someone used us without thought or sympathy, or for blatantly selfish ends, and we are frozen with pain and unable to move ahead as we would like.

With time, but not without considerable patience and effort, most of us will recover. We will never again be the same—we will always be painfully aware of our essential vulnerability, of how our lives can turn on a dime—but we will once again be able to enjoy life and to pursue dreams and ideals that give our existence meaning. "Providence has a thousand ways of raising up the fallen, succoring the weary," wrote Goethe. "Our destiny sometimes has the appearance of a fruit tree in the winter. Looking at its dreary aspect, who would think that these stiff branches, these jagged twigs, will turn green again and bloom next spring and then bear fruit. Yet this we hope, this we know."

*Life begins on the other
side of despair.*
JEAN-PAUL SARTRE

*There is not grief which time
does not lessen and soften.*
CICERO

Sorrow makes us wise.
ALFRED LORD TENNYSON

Many of us, however, are not in life's winter; we are capable of developing our most cherished talents and pursuing our most compelling dreams, yet we refrain from doing so for other reasons. Perhaps we are paralyzed by fear of the unknown, of stepping out and being different, or of failing at something that we know in our hearts to be worthwhile (it is much less painful to fail at something unimportant). Perhaps we are tied down by the unfair expectations of those around us, or shackled by the false values and shallow ideals that we have mistakenly adopted from the world in which we live.

At moments of inspiration, in the soft glow of a winter's evening by the hearth, or during a solitary spring afternoon walk, we catch a glimpse of the greater life that is possible for us. The "still small voice" whispers a dream or an ideal, and we sense that it can be attained, or at least that its pursuit would be both challenging and fulfilling. But later that day or perhaps the next, our vision starts to fade, and a number of smaller events and exigencies flood in to dominate our time and attention. Immersed in the practical, our dreams and aspirations seem uncertain and perhaps a bit foolish. The path with heart, which winds across lush green meadows, through rolling foothills, and up jagged, snow-capped peaks, seems perilous and steep. Although the countryside is rich and beautiful, and although the heights are majestic with clear and spectacular vistas, the path itself seems untrodden and dangerous. We could get lost in the woods or fall from a cliff, or perhaps we could succumb to exposure and fatigue. Certainly, if the

I have no special revelation of God's will. . . . He reveals Himself daily to every human being, but we shut our ears to the "still small voice."

MAHATMA GANDHI

Your soul suffers if you live superficially. People need times in which to concentrate, when they can search their inmost selves. It is tragic that most men have not achieved this feeling of self-awareness. And finally, when they hear the inner voice they do not want to listen anymore. They carry on as before so as not to be constantly reminded of what they have lost.

ALBERT SCHWEITZER

path were a good one, more would have passed this way before, we think, and we hug the ground on which we stand.

The air in the lowlands may be stale and dense, but we are not without company. Many plod the highway of conformity at our side, each following the other in what no one cares to realize is a closed circle. We seek what others seek: comfort, security, money, power, pleasure. But no matter how much of these we attain, we always seem to yearn for more, and a higher part of our nature remains unfulfilled. We are not alone in our conformity; we are only a stranger to our better selves.

In our youth, we start out on this highway with speed and vigor, perhaps expecting it to lead to some permanent respite, a refuge from the struggles of life. We are willing to sell our ideals and trade our greater talents for a success which seems more tangible and secure, a success that can be measured in dollars and cents; we are willing to sacrifice a challenging and fulfilling life today in order to hurry for what we hope will be a life of ease and comfort tomorrow. With age, however, we realize that these goals recede before us like a mirage in the desert. Success and happiness are not distant goals that we suddenly capture and hold, they happen incidentally when we are fulfilling ourselves, when we have found our place and are giving of our most cherished abilities.

The days and weeks pass, however, as we go through our routines, sacrificing the higher part of our nature, our greatest potential for growth and fulfillment,

*Every person must . . . feel a responsibility
to discover his mission in life. God has
given each normal person a capacity
to achieve some end. True, some are
endowed with more talent than others,
but God has left none of us talentless.
Potential powers of creativity are
within us, and we have the duty to work
assiduously to discover these powers.*

MARTIN LUTHER KING, JR.

*There is as much dignity in tilling a field
as in writing a poem.*

BOOKER T. WASHINGTON

to the trivial urgencies that press upon us from all sides. We talk less and less about our forsaken dreams, talents, and ideals, and there exists an unspoken, polite agreement not to trouble others about theirs. The further we get from them, the dimmer they become, until, perhaps, listlessness and boredom set in, and life, to paraphrase Schopenhauer, seems nothing more than the repetition of the same tiresome play. Years leave wrinkles upon the skin, but this loss of enthusiasm, of passion and ideals, wrinkles the soul. Like the timid servant in Jesus' story, we have been thrown into a world of darkness.

We may earn considerable amounts of money and we may try to fill our lives with many fine ornaments and possessions, but something inside remains empty and craving, a question goes unanswered. For once we attain a certain level of comfort and security, it is natural and uniquely human to long for something higher, a sense of purpose, a pursuit which we feel is important, which exercises our most cherished abilities and capacity for service, making us feel a worthwhile part of the world in which we live.

This, in part, is the lesson of the Parable of the Talents, and it is also a truth that has been put forth in other great world religions, philosophies, and contemporary psychological theories. "Do all that is in thine heart, for the Lord is with thee," says the Jewish Torah. "What is the right course that a man should choose for himself?" asks the Talmud. "That which he feels to be honorable to himself, and which also brings him honor

Walk in the ways of thine heart.

ECCLESIASTES 11:9

*Walk in the light of your own fire, and
in the flame which ye have kindled.*

ISAIAH 50:11

*Do all that is in thine heart, for
the Lord is with thee.*

II SAMUEL 7:3

from mankind. . . . Who is honored? He who honors others."

Judaism is profoundly concerned with giving life meaning, with working with God to fulfill His plan, making this world a place of beauty, justice, and truth. Each person plays his part: "It is not upon thee to finish the work," says the Talmud, "neither art thou free to abstain from it." Each of us has a unique role to play in this work. "I am a creature of God and my neighbor is also his creature," says another verse; "my work is in the city and his in the field; I rise early to my work and he rises early to his. As he cannot excel in my work, so I cannot excel in his work. But perhaps you say, I do great things and he does small things! We have learnt that it matters not whether one does much or little if he only directs his heart to Heaven."

Martin Buber, in an inspiring essay on the ways of man according to the teachings of Hasidism, an eighteenth century sect of Judaism which has recently enjoyed a strong revival, writes that "every man's foremost task is the actualization of his unique, unprecedented and never recurring potentialities, and not the repetition of something that another, and be it even the greatest, has already achieved." According to Hasidism, it is through our work and the everyday exercise of our talents that one has access to God. But each person has a different access. "God does not say: 'This way leads to me and that does not,' but he says: 'Whatever you do may be a way to me, provided you do it in such a manner that it leads you to me.' But what it is that can and

No limits are set to the ascent of man,
and the loftiest precincts are open to all.
In this, your choice alone is supreme.

HASIDIC SAYING

Each of us possesses a Holy Spark, but
not everyone exhibits it to best advantage.
It is like the diamond which cannot cast
its luster if buried in the earth. But
when disclosed in its appropriate
setting there is light, as from a
diamond, in each of us.

RABBI ISRAEL OF RIZIN

shall be done by just this person and no other can be revealed to him only in himself . . . only through the knowledge of his own being, the knowledge of his essential quality and inclination. Everyone has in him something precious that is in no one else. But this precious something in a man is revealed to him only if he truly perceives his strongest feeling, his central wish, that in him stirs his inmost being."

Islam, like Judaism and Christianity, the religions from which it springs and which Muslims believe it completes, also stresses that virtue, goodness, and salvation come in part through expressing one's uniqueness and individuality. One of the ways a person does this is through his work and deeds. "To each is a goal to which God turns him," says the Koran. "Then strive together as a race toward all that is good." "When a man dies, they who survive him ask what property he has left behind," says another verse. "The angel who bends over the dying man asks what good deeds he has sent before him." And, "You will never attain righteousness until you give freely of what you love."

In Buddhism, one step in the eightfold path to overcoming life's sufferings and the prison of our own selfishness is through the right livelihood. Our work occupies a great deal of our waking attention, and Buddha considered it impossible to progress spiritually if our occupation pulls us in the opposite direction: "The hand of the dyer is subdued by the dye in which it works." It is therefore imperative that a person get in the right place, a vocation which calls forth his greatest

*Pursue some path, however narrow
and crooked, in which you can
walk with love and reverence.*

HENRY DAVID THOREAU

*What seems different in yourself; that's
the rare thing you possess. The one
thing that gives each of us his worth,
and that's just what we try to suppress.
And we claim to love life.*

ANDRÉ GIDE

love, which connects him with life around him, and which breaks down the hard shell of his ego and his tendency to be a separate entity living only for himself. This right place is unique to each individual. "Let no one forget his own duty," said the Buddha, "For the sake of another's, however great."

Hinduism, like Buddhism, also stresses the importance of doing good works in a spirit of service and sacrifice. But unlike Buddhism, the former religion advocates a tradition of castes, a rigid social system in which people fall into one of four general classes or vocations, not according to their individual talents or inclinations, but according to the family into which they are born. The caste system led former prime minister Jawaharlal Nehru to comment that India is "the least tolerant nation in social forms while the most tolerant in the realm of ideas." This may be true, especially since Hinduism is so very patient with the many different ways or religions by which it believes one may come to know God, and with where an individual may be in his own spiritual quest. ("If we have listening ears, God speaks to us in our own language, whatever that language be," wrote Mahatma Gandhi.)

This paradox of Hinduism notwithstanding, one of the four paths or yogas by which a Hindu may reach God is Karma Yoga. This path stresses the importance of creative action, the manner or spirit in which one lives and discharges his duties. The work one does is not as important as the way in which one does it. The goal, as in Buddhism, is to transcend the smallness of the fi-

*Hide not your talents, they for
use were made.*

BENJAMIN FRANKLIN

*It is the first of all problems for a man
to find out what kind of work he
is to do in this universe.*

THOMAS CARLYLE

*Let no one be like another, yet everyone
like the highest. How is this done?
Be each one perfect in himself.*

JOHANN WOLFGANG VON GOETHE

nite self, and this is done when a person works with love, without thought for personal gain, and in devotion to God. "Do without attachment the work you have to do," says the Bhagavad Gita, "surrendering all action to Me . . . freeing yourself from longing and selfishness." By focusing on God and on service, the Karma Yogi is beyond concern for himself: "One to me is loss and gain,/One to me is fame or shame,/One to me is pleasure, pain." He is serene, focused only on making the work at hand a gift to his beloved God, and this calls out his highest and most noble powers. Like the center of a rapidly spinning wheel, to use a Hindu simile, he remains at rest, even in the midst of concentrated activity.

Confucianism, the great philosophy that for twenty-five hundred years has reflected and shaped the character of China and other nations in the East, also advocates that we make use of our greatest talents and work in a manner which expresses what is highest in our nature. "Wherever you go," said Confucius, "go with your whole heart." His greatest disciple, Mencius (Meng-tsu), wrote: "Those who follow that part of themselves which is great are great men; those who follow that part which is little are little men." Like Socrates in Greece, Confucius practiced what he taught and set an example for others to follow. Although poor and often ridiculed, he would not compromise the ideals or principles by which he lived, even if this meant turning down a comfortable position offered by those in power: "With coarse food to eat, water to drink, and my bent

*Although a man may have no
jurisdiction over the fact of his existence,
he can hold supreme command over
the meaning of existence for him.
Thus no man need fear death; he
need fear only that he may die
without having known his greatest
power—the power of his free will
to give his life for others.*

NORMAN COUSINS

*Not in the clamor of the crowded
street, not in the shouts and plaudits
of the throng, but in ourselves are
triumph and defeat.*

HENRY WADSWORTH LONGFELLOW

arm for a pillow, I still have joy in the midst of these things," he said. "Riches and honors acquired by unrighteousness mean no more to me than floating clouds."

In Western philosophy, Aristotle is the first and foremost advocate of the importance of developing our talents and realizing our highest potential. For Aristotle, man is a rational animal, and like other animals, he has certain physical needs that must be satisfied: the need for food and safety, for example. But what makes man unique, what distinguishes him from other forms of life, is his ability to reason and to contemplate. It is this capacity that must be developed and realized if we are to live well and be fulfilled. "It is what is proper to everyone that is in its nature best and most pleasant for him," says Aristotle. "It is the life that accords with reason that will be best and most pleasant for man, as a man's reason is in the highest sense himself. This will therefore be also the happiest life."

This is not to say that one has to become a philosopher in order to be happy. Aristotle was tolerant enough to recognize that different people have different intellectual and contemplative interests; for example, a person may be interested in medicine, politics, art, engineering, or any other profession that requires some degree of thought and attention. What is important is that one pursue the subject for which he has the greatest affection, for this will lead to the best results. "It is so too with people who are fond of music or architecture or any other subject; their progress in their particular subject is due to the pleasure which they take in it. Plea-

Every industrious man, in every lawful calling, is a useful man. And one principle reason why men are so often useless is that they neglect their own profession or calling, and divide and shift their attention among a multiplicity of objects and pursuits.

RALPH WALDO EMERSON

Our doubts are traitors, and make us lose the good we oft might win by fearing to attempt.

WILLIAM SHAKESPEARE

sure helps increase activity," and there is an intimate connection between pleasure and the "activity which it perfects."

American philosopher Ralph Waldo Emerson also stresses the importance of pursuing work in which we have a particular interest or which gives us pleasure. "The high prize of life, the crowning fortune of a man, is to be born with a bias to some pursuit which finds him in employment and happiness." In his essay "Self-Reliance," Emerson emphasizes the importance of following one's own heart, of developing one's most unique talents and most cherished abilities: "There is a time in every man's education when he arrives at the conviction that envy is ignorance; that imitation is suicide; that he must take himself for better or worse as his portion; that though the wide universe is full of good, no kernel of nourishing corn can come to him but through his toil bestowed on that plot of ground which is given him to till. The power which resides in him is new in nature, and none but he knows what that is which he can do, nor does he know until he has tried."

Contemporary psychology is also rich in writings on the importance of developing our talents and pursuing our highest ideals. "There is no meaning to life except the meaning that man gives his life by the unfolding of his powers," writes Erich Fromm. Erik Erikson states, "Although aware of the relativity of all the various life styles which give meaning to human striving, the possessor of integrity is ready to defend the dignity of his own life style against all physical and economic

*All serious success in work depends upon
some genuine interest in the material
with which the work is concerned.*

BERTRAND RUSSELL

*A happy life is one which is in
accordance with its own nature.*

SENECA

*To be what we are, and to become
what we are capable of becoming,
is the only end in life.*

BARUCH SPINOZA

threats." And Rollo May observes, "If any organism fails to fulfill its potentialities, it becomes sick, just as your legs would wither if you never walked. But the power of your legs is not all you would lose. The flowing of your blood, your heart action, your whole organism would be the weaker. And in the same way if man does not fulfill his potentialities as a person, he becomes to that extent constricted and ill."

Abraham Maslow devoted his career to studying what he called the "peak performers," that small segment of the population which progressively actualizes its talents and capabilities. He believed that the average person is motivated primarily by deficiencies; that is, by trying to fulfill his most basic needs for food and safety, belongingness and affection, respect and self-esteem. While these needs are satisfied, however, the healthy person is "motivated by his need to develop and actualize his fullest potentialities and capacities." He has a sense of purpose or "mission," and he continually strives to realize certain values which he holds dear through his work and conduct. If a person ignores his higher needs (which Maslow believed are just as important to a person's total well-being as the basic needs), then he will never be fulfilled or at peace with himself. "If you deliberately plan to be less than you are capable of being, then I warn you that you'll be unhappy for the rest of your life. You will be evading your own capacities, your own possibilities."

Finally, Viktor Frankl, a survivor of Aushwitz and founder of logotherapy, the third Viennese school of

Every man hath his proper gift of God, one after this manner and another after that.

I CORINTHIANS 7:7

Be watchful, stand firm in your faith, be courageous, be strong. Let all that you do be done in love.

I CORINTHIANS 16:13–14

psychotherapy, believes that man's primary motivation is not pleasure, as Freud believed, or the will to power, as Adler believed (basing his psychology on Nietzsche), but the will to meaning. What a person wants most, what he is even willing to die for, is for his life to be meaningful, significant. One of the ways in which we can make our lives meaningful is through our work and the manner in which we carry out the tasks and responsibilities before us. "With his unique destiny each man stands, so to speak, alone in the entire cosmos. His destiny will not recur. No one else has the same potentialities as he, nor will he himself be given them again." The concrete task of each individual is relative to his uniqueness and singularity; "the radius of the activity is not important; important alone is whether he fills the circle of his task." Mental health, according to Frankl, "is based on a certain degree of tension, the tension between what one has already achieved and what one still ought to accomplish, or the gap between what one is and what one should become." Remarkably, Frankl found, through his dreadful experience as a prisoner of war, that this tension can even be a matter of life and death. "In the Nazi concentration camps," he writes, "one could have witnessed that those who knew that there was a task waiting for them to fulfill were most apt to survive." Quoting Nietzsche's aphorism, "He who has a why to live for can bear with almost any how," Frankl credits his own survival, particularly with a near-fatal bout with typhus fever, to his desire to rewrite a

Each act of unfaithfulness toward our inner being is a blot on our souls. If we continue to be unfaithful, our souls are eventually torn apart and we slowly bleed to death. Harmony and strength exist in our lives only when our outer selves match our inner selves, when this great truthfulness forges an inner harmony between our deepest and purest yearnings and the goals we pursue in life.

ALBERT SCHWEITZER

manuscript which the Nazis had confiscated when he entered the camp.

With so many voices of wisdom—the great writers, thinkers, and spiritual leaders of the ages—counseling us to develop our most cherished talents, to express our uniqueness and individuality, and to make our work a gift to God and to the world in which we live, why do so many of us settle for less? Why are we compelled to hang upon the coast, exploring shallow waters, swinging safely at anchor, or sinking our keel into riches and pleasures, when we could set sail for the not-so-distant shores of our greatest potential, for the unexplored lands of our fondest dreams?

II

LIVES OF QUIET

DESPERATION

———

Many of us are aware that a greater life is possible. We sense that we have scarcely realized our potential, our powers, and that there lie vast continents, strange and wonderful worlds of unexplored territory within. "Compared to what we ought to be," wrote William James, "we are only half awake. Our fires are damped, our drafts are checked, we are making use of only a small part of our mental and physical resources."

In looking back, we can remember times when we were rewarded for exploring our talents, for taking risks, either by getting what we wanted or by learning in the process. Everything we can do, all the skills we possess, came from taking chances, from finding the courage to gingerly test the chill waters of the unknown. Learning to walk and talk, to read and write, to understand and get along with others, to cope with our disappointments and losses, discovering our love for music, art, literature,

*Although men are accused of not
knowing their own weakness, yet
perhaps few know their own strength.
It is in men as in soils, where
sometimes there is a vein of gold
which the owner knows not of.*

JONATHAN SWIFT

*Great spirits are not those who have
fewer passions and greater virtue
than ordinary men, but only
those who have the greatest aims.*

LA ROCHEFOUCAULD

science, crafts, or athletics—everything we have accomplished and learned, as individuals and as a race, has come from our willingness to reach beyond ourselves. Without this willingness we would neither have matured nor survived.

Yet, as we grow older, something often begins to hold us back. We become increasingly afraid of falling down, of appearing foolish or getting hurt. The sorrows and disappointments of life erode our strength as water crumbles stone. Looking around, we see those few unbroken souls who have managed to hold on to their ideals, to take risks and explore their most cherished talents and abilities. The scientist who, after many years, makes a startling breakthrough that saves lives or helps us understand our world. The artist who creates a beautiful song, poem, or picture that awakens our soul, and makes us grateful to be alive. The athlete who reminds us of the strength, endurance, and remarkable agility of the human body. The innovator who, despite the odds, brings a valuable product or service to market, and we wonder how we ever managed without it. In many cases, these people are rewarded for their respective excellence, materially, financially, with recognition from their peers and admiration from others. More importantly, however, their lives have elements of passion and excitement, meaning and fulfillment, that are often lacking in the lives of those who will not or cannot be true to their higher calling.

It is tempting to imagine that those who achieve greatness, in whatever measure, within whatever radius

*Once you say you're going to settle
for second, that's what happens
to you in life, I find.*

JOHN F. KENNEDY

*to be nobody but yourself—in a world
which is doing its best, night and day,
to make you like everybody else—
means to fight the hardest battle
which any human being can fight,
and never stop fighting*

e. e. cummings

of activity, had decisive advantages at the start. We often think that they somehow had means and opportunities that are unavailable to most. But seldom is this true. Charles Dickens was pulled out of school at the age of twelve to support himself by working in a shoe-polish factory while his parents were in debtors' prison. Grandma Moses spent her life on a farm, raising ten children, before taking up painting at the age of seventy-eight, when her arthritic hands could no longer hold an embroidery needle; by the time she was ninety, her paintings were known and loved worldwide. Abraham Lincoln walked for miles with legendary resolve just to borrow a book. "I will study and get ready, and perhaps my chance will come," he said. Helen Keller lost her sight, hearing, and ability to speak, and yet went on to graduate with honors from Radcliff, to write several books, to lecture, and to inspire people everywhere not to feel sorry for themselves but to make the most of what they have. "Life is either a daring adventure or nothing," she said.

Nor do people who live extraordinary lives necessarily have an easy path. No one rolls stones out of their way; more likely than not, others may even try to block their passage. Mahatma Gandhi was imprisoned numerous times in his struggle to lead India, in nonviolence, to independence, and he ultimately died trying to unite the nation torn by sectarian hate. Martin Luther King, Jr., was repeatedly threatened (along with his wife and children), had his house firebombed, was imprisoned nineteen times for standing up nonviolently to unjust

*Few will have the greatness to bend
history itself, but each of us can work
to change a small portion of events. . . . It
is from numberless acts of courage and
belief that human history is shaped.*

ROBERT KENNEDY

*The most acceptable service to
God is doing good to man.*

BENJAMIN FRANKLIN

*There is no road too long to the man
who advances deliberately and without
undue haste; no honors too distant to
the man who prepares himself for
them with patience.*

LA BRUYÈRE

laws, but pressed on in love and faith, even when he had an uncanny premonition of his own death. Albert Schweitzer left a comfortable life as a university professor and parish minister to return to medical school; then, upon completion of his studies, at the age of thirty-eight, he traveled to the African Congo, where he cleared the forest and built a hospital with his bare hands, and served people who would otherwise have suffered and died of preventable causes, for over fifty years. Mother Teresa also left a comfortable life as a teacher at the convent in Loretto at the age of thirty-eight, to travel alone to Calcutta, without any idea of where or how to begin, because she felt called to make God's love manifest in action, by serving the poorest of the poor. Those who knew her in Loretto say that they had no idea of her strength and determination; she had always seemed so meek and delicate in comparison with others.

None of these individuals had any particular advantages. None of them had it easy. Their lives are evidence that there is no progress without struggle, no growth without uncertainty, no victory without the willingness to risk defeat. Something inside gave them strength, enabled them to press onward to their personal summit when most others would want to turn back. Their hearts were full of love for life and for their fellowman. They had faith in God and in the God-given abilities. They had hope that with sacrifice and effort, they or anyone else can make a difference in the world, not necessarily by grand gesture or newsworthy feat, but by small acts, done patiently and with care.

Lives of great men all remind us
We can make our lives sublime,
And, departing, leave behind us,
Footprints on the sands of time. . . .

Let us, then, be up and doing,
With a heart for any fate;
Still achieving, still pursuing,
Learn to labor and to wait.

HENRY WADSWORTH LONGFELLOW

What we nourish in ourselves grows—
such is the everlasting law of nature.

JOHANN WOLFGANG VON GOETHE

The lives of these men and women, the example of their courage and faith, make us feel that we, too, are capable of something extraordinary, of leaving our "footprints on the sands of time." We recognize in those who realize their talents and abilities, who leave their indelible gift to the world, that part of ourselves which also can be great. We know, at the very core of our being, where truth and faith have not been marred by the falseness and cynicism of the world, that we can do something exceptional. It doesn't have to be on a grand scale, but where we are, with what we have, we can make the most of ourselves and give something of value to the world. Perhaps our duty lies in educating ourselves, in further preparing for the tests and opportunities that lie ahead; perhaps there is a way, through our work and relations, to make this world a little safer, more honest and caring; perhaps there is someone who depends on us whose life we can touch. Discovering our purpose and then striving to fulfill it gives our lives meaning and satisfaction unknown to those who pursue a more shallow version of success.

Sometimes, however, our calling is faint. Many of us are presently unable to move forward because life has dealt us a severe or tragic blow, and we are reeling in confusion and despair. Our energies are consumed and depressed; the "still small voice" that once urged us to do the greater thing is now scarcely audible, deadened by our pain. Perhaps we are enduring a loss or a personal tragedy: the death of a loved one, a failed relationship, poor health, the loss of a job, dream, or ideal. It is

*When sorrows come, they come not
as single spies, but in battalions!*
WILLIAM SHAKESPEARE

*Even in the deepest sinking there is
the hidden purpose of an ultimate
rising. Thus it is for men; from none
is the source of light withheld
unless he himself withdraws from it.
Therefore the most important
thing is not to despair.*
HASIDIC SAYING

hard to think about living an extraordinary life, of reaching for the heights of our potential, of seizing the day to partake of life's beauty and joy, when there is so much hurt inside. It is all we can do just to cope with the demands of daily living. We find ourselves on a frozen and desolate plain, struggling to keep moving or to set up camp so as not to succumb to the cold.

In the midst of such despair, we wonder if we will ever again feel warmth and see light. Forlornly, we recall the way things were before our present crisis, our passion, our sense of purpose, our ability to enjoy the sweetness and fullness of existence—will these treasures ever be regained? Will we ever again be able to love and feel deeply, to overcome our numbness? Will we ever again have the faith and energy to do the things that we dream? The answer is yes, we will, but with much patience and gentle effort. Also, hopefully, with the support of those willing to give us strength by sharing our pain—family, friends, clergy, competent professionals. There is a season for everything, and like all seasons, the season for healing must run its course. There is no measuring progress in days or weeks or even months, only by our ability to gradually regain what is best in ourselves.

Rabbi Pesach Krauss, former chaplain at Memorial Sloan-Kettering Cancer Center in New York, where he counseled patients and their families, tells an inspiring parable in his book *Why Me?* Two woodchoppers have cut down a tree that is well over a hundred years old. The younger man, observing the tree's growth rings,

You cannot prevent the birds of sadness
from passing over your head,
but you can prevent them
from nesting in your hair.

CHINESE PROVERB

We need to get over the questions that
focus on the past and on the pain—
"Why did this happen to me?"—
and ask instead the question which
opens doors to the future: "Now that
this has happened, what shall
I do about it?"

RABBI HAROLD KUSHNER

remarks that five of the rings are very close together. There must have been a five-year drought, he concludes, during which the tree experienced very little growth. The older timberman, however, known for his gentle wisdom, has a different perspective. The dry years were actually the most important years of the tree's life, he contends. Because of the drought, the tree had to force its roots deeper and deeper into the soil, in order to get the water and nourishment it needed. Then, when conditions improved, it was able to grow taller and faster because of its strengthened roots.

Likewise, our difficult times, the times when we are coping with loss or tragedy, can be times of great inner growth. Words cannot adequately describe the pain we may be enduring. Our emotional and spiritual suffering can be every bit as real and debilitating as physical injury, and this is often difficult for others to recognize or understand. Yet with patient work, and faith in a better tomorrow, we will pass through our crisis, leaving one phase of our lives, but entering another which is bright and laden with potential. We will never be the same person we were before, but with our renewed strength and deepened sensitivity, we will be able to move on to new areas of growth, experience, and fulfillment. "There is a budding morrow in midnight," wrote John Keats. "The lowest ebb is the turn of the tide," observed Longfellow. "The world breaks everyone," said Hemingway, "and afterward many are strong in the broken places."

For some the process of healing will be more

We are healed of a suffering only by experiencing it to the full.

MARCEL PROUST

Problems call forth our courage and our wisdom; indeed, they create our courage and our wisdom. It is only because of problems that we grow mentally and spiritually.

M. SCOTT PECK

lengthy and difficult than for others. Some people were injured early in life, though the pain and awareness of this injustice may only be surfacing now. Someone, perhaps someone very close to them who was charged with their care, hurt or abused them, physically, emotionally. All of their lives they have lacked courage and faith in themselves because their sense of worth was damaged at an early age. The world, for them, is a dangerous place, and they have learned that it is safer not to take risks, not to call attention to themselves.

Jesus admonished anyone who would harm a child that it is better that he tie a millstone around his neck and throw himself into the sea. Yet, tragically, many children are harmed, wittingly or unwittingly, by those who should cherish and protect them. This is the source of much of the world's suffering. It makes it difficult for many to open their hearts and to trust in all that is good in life. Furthermore, it is difficult or impossible for people to realize their talents and potentialities when their sense of value, as human beings who have needs and feelings of their own, has been selfishly violated. "Self-trust is the first secret of success," says Emerson. "Public opinion is a weak tyrant compared with our own private opinion," states Thoreau. "The pious and just honoring of ourselves may be thought the fountainhead from whence every laudable and worthy enterprise issues forth," writes Milton.

How can people in this situation, or any of us who have suffered a loss of self-esteem, regain our birthright, our sense of worth, our awareness of our wonderful gifts

When a man suffers, he ought not to
say, "That's bad! That's bad!"
Nothing that God imposes on man
is bad. But it is all right to say,
"That's bitter!" For among medicines
there are some that are made
with bitter herbs.
HASIDIC SAYING

It is one of life's laws that as soon as
one door closes, another one opens.
But the tragedy is that we look at the
closed door and disregard the open one.
ANDRÉ GIDE

and potentialities? There are no easy answers, and for each of us the work that needs to be done will be necessarily different. Certainly, a first and important step is to seek the community of others who "bear the mark of pain." Their fellowship will be a source of strength and encouragement. We will realize that we are not alone in our suffering and that progress is indeed possible. Beyond this, however, we must realize that spiritual and emotional healing, like physical healing, is gradual and best taken in small steps. Choose each day to do some small thing that affirms what you know to be true; that you are valuable, that you have an indomitable spirit that is capable of great love and happiness. Read a book that fills you with hope, listen to music that soothes your soul, take care of yourself by eating well, getting fresh air, rest, and exercise. Make small decisions that silently claim your right to follow your own heart. In time, these decisions will lead to greater ones that will also affirm your worth. Furthermore, you will draw courage and satisfaction from knowing that your life is directed toward wholeness and well-being. The important thing is not so much where we stand, it has been said, but in what direction our life is moving.

For some of us, therefore, the task of the moment is to heal, to regain our sense of value and confidence. Though we may presently be unable to develop our unique talents, to pursue our special dream, God may have given us another challenge which is no less important and which also demands patience and effort. "Every man shall bear his own burden," said the Apostle Paul,

*We must learn to endure what we
cannot avoid. Our life is composed, like
the harmony of the world, of contrary
things, also of different tones, sweet
and harsh, sharp and flat, soft and loud.
If a musician liked only one kind,
what would he have to say? He must
know how to use them together
and blend them.*

MICHEL DE MONTAIGNE

*God grant me the serenity to accept the
things I cannot change, the courage to
change the things I can, and the
wisdom to know the difference.*

THE SERENITY PRAYER

and perhaps your burden at this time is to regain what is best in yourself. Though it might feel as if you have fallen off the path which leads to your most worthy ideals, the truth is you that have not fallen off the path at all. You are only passing through a dark and shadowy valley, a particularly difficult and challenging part of your journey. You must find the courage to take the next step, however small and tentative, and then the next. Your destiny may turn out to be greater than you imagined.

Many of us, however, are not passing through the darkness of a personal crisis or tragedy. We have survived our loss, we have grown through our pain. We have reasonable confidence in ourselves and in our ability to affect the world in which we live. But still we do not act. Though able to hear the "still small voice" that urges us to reach for our dream, or to grow and blossom where we have already been sown, we do not answer the calling. We do not take the requisite step of faith and make our necessary parting with the crowd.

Instead, we do what is common, yielding to our natural inclination for ease and comfort (goals which Albert Einstein commented are "more proper for a herd of swine"), or we do what others say we should do, displacing what we value by giving importance to what others or society in general seems to value: financial and material prosperity, power, and position. One finds it "too venturesome a thing to be himself," observed Søren Kierkegaard, "far easier to be an imitation, a number, a cipher in the crowd." As a result, we live in a

*Why should we be in such desperate
haste to succeed and in such desperate
enterprises? If a man does not keep pace
with his companions, perhaps it is
because he hears a different drummer.
Let him step to the music which he
hears, however measured or far away.*

HENRY DAVID THOREAU

*To act without clear understanding,
to form habits without investigation,
to follow a path all one's life without
knowing where it really leads,
such is the behavior of the multitude.*

MENCIUS

prison of our own making. We set our own limits and wittingly hold ourselves back from the richer and fuller life, from the greater sense of adventure and satisfaction, that is possible for us. And, tragically, we deprive the world, those with whom our invaluable, brief existence comes into contact, of our most sincere gift. In a sense, a part of us dies before our death.

In his short novel *The Death of Ivan Ilyich*, Leo Tolstoy tells the story of a man whose chief ambitions in life have been wealth, power, and the esteem of the upper class. In pursuit of these, he sacrifices his own dreams and convictions, and adopts the ideals and values of those whom he so much admires. In effect, he becomes a stranger to himself, losing touch with important facets of his personality, replacing the true with the false. "All of the passion of youth and childhood had passed away," writes Tolstoy, "not leaving serious traces."

On his deathbed, it occurs to Ivan that even though he has been successful in terms of wealth and position, even though he has bought the right furniture and invited the right people to his house for dinner, maybe his life has really been a failure. " 'Maybe I did not live as I ought to have done,' it suddenly occurred to him. 'But how can that be, when I did everything properly?' he replied, and immediately dismissed from his mind this, the sole solution of life and death, as something quite impossible." But the terrible thought keeps coming back. Perhaps he did not live his life in the right way; perhaps success is something different than he had

*What I must do is all that concerns me,
not what the people think. This rule,
equally arduous in actual and in
intellectual life, may serve for the
whole distinction between greatness
and meanness. It is the harder because
you will always find those who think
they know what is your duty better
than you know it. It is easy in the world
to live after the world's opinion; it is easy
in solitude to live after our own; but the
great man is he who in the midst of the
crowd keeps with perfect sweetness
the independence of solitude.*

RALPH WALDO EMERSON

thought. " 'It was as if I had been going downhill while I imagined I was going up. And that is really what it was. I was going up in public opinion, but to the same extent life was ebbing away from me. And now it is all done and there is only death.' "

Could it be that many of us are going downhill when we think we are going up? Could the passion and ideals, the talents and dreams, the raw sensitivity of our youth, be slipping away from us as we adopt the values and goals of those around us? What makes Ivan's situation tragic, and his death agonizing, is that he does not realize the falseness of his life until it is practically too late. But we may be more fortunate. There may still be time to turn from mediocrity and conformity, from laziness and fear, and to follow the path with heart. We may yet have the chance to express greater love and originality in the place where we stand, or, if we are so inclined, to take small steps—if not a giant leap—toward our most cherished dreams and aspirations.

In our youth, we are passionate for all that is good in the world, sensitive to all that could be better. Our emotions are raw and tingle on the surface of our being. A beautiful song can bring us to tears, a statement of truth can pierce our hearts; suffering elicits our deepest sympathy, injustice our most scalding enmity and indignation. We feel ourselves to be in touch with God and with our fellowman. We are participants in the world and our lives stretch out before us, lined with abundant possibilities.

As we grow older, however, the ideals and convic-

Adults are only too partial to the sorry task of warning youth that some day they will view most of the things that now inspire their hearts and minds as mere illusions. But those who have a deeper experience of life take another tone. They exhort youth to try to preserve throughout their lives the ideas that inspire them. In youthful idealism man perceives the truth. In youthful idealism he possesses riches that should not be bartered for anything on earth.

ALBERT SCHWEITZER

tions that are precious to us in youth may be steadily dissolved by the hardships and exigencies of existence. A man "once believed in the victory of truth," observed Schweitzer, "now he no longer does. He believed in humanity; that is over. He believed in the Good; that is over. He eagerly sought justice; that is over. He trusted in the power of kindness and peaceableness; that is over. In order to steer more safely through the perils and storms of life, he has lightened his boat. He has thrown overboard goods that he considered dispensable. But the ballast he dumped was actually his food and drink. Now he skims more lightly over the waves, but he is hungry and parched."

Holding on to our ideals and convictions is perhaps the most difficult thing any of us can do. Inevitably, we run up against hardships and obstacles in life that tempt us to abandon what we know to be right and to take an easier way. A young woman who wants to be a doctor decides that the years of hard work and rigorous training are too much to bear, and she takes an easier job that for her has little meaning and does not make use of her special gifts. A young man gives up on his dream to compose or perform music, to partake in one of humanity's most beautiful achievements, because his family or friends staunchly remind him of the pitfalls and dangers of an artist's career. Still another person, perhaps a bit older, decides to compromise his sense of values—values which once gave his life meaning—in order to make a quick profit or to enjoy some fleeting pleasure or illicit return. "It's what everyone

The youth gets together his materials to build a bridge to the moon, or perchance a palace or temple on the earth, and at length the middle-aged man concludes to build a woodshed with them.

HENRY DAVID THOREAU

Our heart changes, and this is the greatest cause of suffering in life.

MARCEL PROUST

else does," he rationalizes. "I'm only human. Nobody's perfect."

It is a sorry day when we give up what is best in ourselves, when we sacrifice the values and ideals that give our lives meaning, for some temporary advantage. In doing so we lose something more precious than anything that we could possibly gain, and we create an emptiness in the pit of our being which becomes difficult to fill. Like a house left empty, a life devoid of purpose and values has a way of deteriorating and growing musty with time. Far better to keep our lives lighted with hope, alive with creative activity, and open to the fresh air of worthwhile ideals.

This is challenging, in part, because, as we grow up, there is the constant pressure to conform, to fit in. From our earliest years, we want to be liked, we want to be part of the group. This is human; we need each other deeply. What is more, being an outcast is painful, and others can be shockingly cruel and adept at administering the pain. Consequently, we sometimes make the mistake of smoothing out the edges of our personality in order to be accepted. We chip and sand away at our truest values, at our most cherished ideals, and then add others that fit poorly in their place, because we are justifiably afraid of standing alone. Tragically, however, if others accept or admire the person we have created, we still are not at ease. They accept an image we present, not us; they admire a counterfeit person, an imposter, not the person we know in our hearts we are or can be. Thus our conformity is self-defeating. Even in suc-

*The supreme happiness of life is the
conviction of being loved for yourself,
or, more correctly, being loved
in spite of yourself.*

VICTOR HUGO

*It is better to fail in originality
than to succeed in imitation.*

HERMAN MELVILLE

cess we feel like a failure. Even with others we feel alone. True community, true love and acceptance, can only be born of truth.

Some writers, particularly Nietzsche, have looked upon conformity and even the spirit of constructive co-operation as emasculating influences that stunt the growth and inhibit the power of the world's most noble and courageous spirits. In one startling aphorism, he claims that all truly great lives have been like glaciers that have cut their way across mountains, reducing to rubble everything that stands in their way, first being agents of destruction. But sometime later, grass, wild-flowers, and trees spring from the ground, and the treacherous path cut by the glacier becomes a beautiful, verdant valley, nourished by rich soil and flowing streams, bursting with life.

Like a glacier, Nietzsche calls on his reader to be willing to destroy the norms and culture in which he lives, to break away from the "herd" and to live by his own standard, even if this is considered evil. The meta-phor is striking, and perhaps there is a drop of truth to it, albeit in a poisonous lake. The artist Picasso re-marked, "Every act of creation is first of all an act of destruction." And Rollo May writes, "Whenever there is a breakthrough of a significant idea in science or a significant new form in art, the new idea will destroy what a lot of people believe is essential to the survival of their intellectual and spiritual world." But there is an obvious danger to the course advocated by Nietzsche, because, if our foremost concern is not for the well-

An individual has not started living until he can rise above the narrow confines of his individualistic concerns to the broader concerns of all humanity.

MARTIN LUTHER KING, JR.

A successful man is he who receives a great deal from his fellow man; usually incomparably more than corresponds to his service to them. The value of a man, however, should be seen in what he gives and not in what he is able to receive.

ALBERT EINSTEIN

being of our fellowman and the world in which we live, if we are motivated by the desire to destroy rather than to build, by power and selfishness rather than by love and what Schweitzer called reverence for life, then almost any action can be justified, even the heinous acts of a Hitler or a Stalin. There would be little chance of our survival; and, indeed, there would be little for which to survive.

Our independence must therefore be tempered, paradoxically, by dependence. Our need to stand alone by our need to stand together. Our desire to break away by our desire to mend and make whole. "If I am not for myself, who will be for me? And being for myself, what am I?" asks the Talmud. "We are called to be individuals. We are called to be unique and different," writes M. Scott Peck in *The Different Drum*, ". . . yet the reality is that we are inevitably social creatures who desperately need each other not merely for sustenance, not merely for company, but for any meaning to our lives whatsoever."

Unfortunately, even if you have a dream that could benefit others, even if you have a vision of a better world and are willing to endure the pain that inevitably accompanies growth and the insecurity that inevitably accompanies going forth into the unknown, the people in your life may feel uncomfortable and try to persuade you to remain where you are. They may ridicule you or be all too willing to remind you of your limits and the dangers of the path you wish to follow. Albert Schweitzer's family tried to call his attention to the "folly" of his desire

*Great Spirits have always encountered
violent opposition from mediocre minds.*

ALBERT EINSTEIN

*You can't hold a man down
without staying down with him.*

BOOKER T. WASHINGTON

*I long to accomplish a great and noble task,
but it is my chief duty to accomplish small tasks
as if they were great and noble.*

HELEN KELLER

to serve as a doctor in Africa. Anton Dvorak's father tried to persuade his son to become a butcher rather than a composer. Handel's father reportedly wanted him to be a lawyer; Cézanne's, a businessman. Isaac Newton's mother wanted him to run the family farm and did not like his reading so many books. Florence Nightingale's family thought it better that she get married and live a quiet and comfortable life rather than enter the profession of nursing, which at the time was disreputable.

Why is this? Why do those around us, sometimes those closest in our lives, often try to hold us back from fulfilling our highest potential? Perhaps, in part, because in pursuing our dreams, we remind them, consciously or unconsciously, of their forsaken ideals, of their undeveloped talents; maybe they want everyone and everything around them, insofar as possible, to validate their own choices, their own path in life. Or perhaps they are genuinely concerned that we may suffer or fail, not realizing that the pursuit of our dreams and the progressive realization of our talents, even though they may not make us a lot of money or always produce the results we desire, is success, and that fear, following the wrong path, or trying to stay where we are, no matter how comfortable and secure we may be, is failure. Or perhaps they are afraid of change. Life can be confusing and maybe they want their world, and the people in it, to somehow stand still and to be understandable, to fit neatly into their conception of things. What they do not realize is that to develop our talents, to make use of our

Keep away from people who try to belittle your ambitions. Small people always do that, but the really great make you feel that you, too, can become great.

MARK TWAIN

He labors vainly, who endeavors to please every person.

LATIN PROVERB

greatest abilities, it is necessary to change, it is necessary to move step by step from the plains of mediocrity and further up the path with heart, to the glorious peaks where we have a clearer view of life and of ourselves. As philosopher Henri Bergson wrote, "To change is to mature, and to mature is to go on creating oneself endlessly."

How can we stand up to the forces that oppose us? How can we win over the people who want us to live in accordance with their values and ideals rather than with our own, and yet not sever the ties of love and the bonds of sympathy that are so vital to our health and well-being? The answer lies in the tradition of civil disobedience practiced by Socrates, Jesus, Mahatma Gandhi, and Martin Luther King, Jr. If others stand in our way, it is counterproductive to meet them with violence, whether this violence be physical or emotional. We may gain the world, but lose our soul. However, neither should we give in or acquiesce to what we know is wrong; rather, we must resist their injustice with all the force of our being, opposing them with love and understanding, with a willingness to suffer and endure rather than resort to violence or submit to their will.

"The old law of an eye for an eye leaves everyone blind," wrote Martin Luther King, Jr. "It is immoral because it seeks to humiliate the opponent rather than win his understanding; it seeks to annihilate rather than to convert. Violence is immoral because it thrives on hatred rather than love. It destroys community and makes brotherhood impossible. It leaves society in a

*Thank not those faithful who praise
all thy words and actions, but those
who kindly reprove thy faults.*

SOCRATES

*Have you learned lessons only of those
who admire you, and were tender with
you, and stood aside for you? Have you
not learned great lessons from those
who rejected you, and braced
themselves against you, or disputed the
passage with you?*

WALT WHITMAN

monologue rather than a dialogue. Violence ends by defeating itself. It creates bitterness in survivors and brutality in destroyers." And in another passage he states, "The non-violent approach does not immediately change the heart of the oppressor. It first does something to the hearts and souls of those committed to it. It gives them new self respect; it calls up resources of strength and courage that they did not know they had. Finally, it reaches the opponent and so stirs his conscience that reconciliation becomes a reality."

If our path is blocked, we must resist those who block it with love, patience, and understanding. Perhaps they have good reason, and we can learn from them. However, if the path we wish to follow is right, and if we resist the forces that oppose us in the spirit of friendship and civility—but resist them nonetheless with all of the strength in our being, with what Gandhi called *satyagraha*, meaning "the force of love and truth"—then others will come to see the validity of our vision, and in admiration for our determination, in compassion for our willingness to suffer for what we know is right, they may even become allies and support us in our cause.

But nonviolent resistance is not a way for the weak. It is likely to require more strength, determination, and patience than anything we have ever done before. And there are other factors that make it difficult. One is that from birth we are taught to be obedient and to seek the approval of others, starting with our parents, and this makes standing on our own particularly difficult. For a period of time longer than that of any other species, we

This is in essence the principle of non-violent non-cooperation. It follows therefore that it must have its roots in love. Its object should not be to punish the opponent or to inflict injury upon him. Even while non-cooperating with him, we must make him feel that in us he has a friend, and we should try to reach his heart by rendering him humanitarian service whenever possible.

MAHATMA GANDHI

are, as infants, entirely dependent on our parents for survival. When we do something of which they do not approve, we are often scolded or punished; when we do something of which they do approve, the care, love, and affection which we so desperately need are given to us. Thus we come to associate our parents' disapproval with feeling bad and their approval with feeling good. Parents have the difficult task of caring for and loving their children while eventually fostering the autonomy and self-reliance that will be necessary for their continued growth and fulfillment later in life.

As we get older, passing from childhood into adolescence and early adulthood, we gradually learn to make our own decisions and to sometimes stand apart from our parents. But some of us get stuck on our need for approval, and we may eventually rely on our boss, a teacher, our spouse, or someone else who has power and authority in our lives, to accept and commend us for our decisions and their consequences. We are afraid of standing on our own, of deciding for ourselves, so we transfer responsibility to someone else. Ironically, however, in giving someone else responsibility for our lives, we have essentially made a decision.

Even away from home, in school, we are taught to be obedient and to seek approval, in the form of good grades, rather than to be independent and to think for ourselves. Albert Einstein once said, "It is nothing short of a miracle that modern methods of instruction have not already completely strangled the holy curiosity of inquiry, because what this delicate little plant needs

What does education often do? It makes a straight-cut ditch of a free, meandering brook.

HENRY DAVID THOREAU

If a man empties his purse into his head, no one can take it away from him. An investment in knowledge always pays the best interest.

BENJAMIN FRANKLIN

most, apart from initial stimulus, is freedom; without this it is surely destroyed." Indeed, our education should foster independence and creativity, understanding and tolerance, and a love and fascination with the hard-won wisdom and experience of our fellowman. Instead, it is often a plethora of facts and figures that we have to memorize in order to do well on a test. As a result, we often do not learn to reason for ourselves; we have a collection of recipes, but we never take the time to prepare and enjoy them, or to add to them according to our own experience and tastes. We finish school pretty much thinking (or not thinking) the same as everyone else.

There are, to be sure, many excellent teachers who foster understanding and creativity and who plant the seeds of intellectual curiosity that will grow and blossom in the student for the rest of his life; the fault, in many cases, lies with the student himself. If he wants a good education, there are ample resources; he need only borrow or buy a book from his local library or bookstore, and then spend an afternoon or an evening in the company of, for example, Shakespeare or Tolstoy, Gandhi or King, reveling in the sweet harmony and cadence of their language, listening to the carefully distilled ideas which they discovered and found important enough to transfer from their minds to paper, and thinking critically about how these ideas apply to his experiences and perceptions. "The true university of these days is a collection of books," wrote Carlyle. "I never let schooling interfere with my education," commented Mark Twain.

*A book is the precious lifeblood
of a master spirit.*
JOHN MILTON

Books are nourishment to the mind.
ITALIAN PROVERB

*Some books are to be tasted, others
to be swallowed, and some few to be
chewed and digested.*
FRANCIS BACON

Or, if a young person is more interested in non-intellectual pursuits, there are many other ways to learn. For example, he might volunteer several hours a week in order to learn a skill or trade that is particularly suited to his temperament, working as a mechanic, a carpenter, a painter, a secretary, or as a gardener, a cook, or any of scores of other noble possibilities. A healthy society recognizes that there are many different ways to express excellence and that all of them are important. It gives young people the opportunity to discover and develop their unique talents, knowing that this is where they can make their greatest contribution, and endeavors to afford them every advantage to excel at that which they choose to do.

Discovering precisely what it is we wish to do with our lives is, however, no easy task. It requires continued discipline and resolve, for a person, young or old, to distance himself from the negative influences in his environment, from the constant noise and banter of the world in which we live, and to be alone and in perfect stillness with the dictates of his soul. But this is precisely what is necessary if we are to hear our higher calling and follow the path with heart. Our modern world is so busy, so restless and full of activity, that it has become increasingly difficult for us to find the peace and tranquillity that are necessary to be in touch with the higher part of our own nature and to contemplate the course of our short and unrepeatable lives. French historian de Toqueville, upon traveling in the United States over one hundred and fifty years ago, wrote that he had

*Learning is an ornament in prosperity,
a refuge in adversity, and a
provision in old age.*

ARISTOTLE

*Who is wise? He who learns
from all men.*

BEN ZOMA

(ETHICS OF THE FATHERS)

never seen a less philosophical society: "Their life is so practical, so confused, so excited, so active, that little time remains to them for thought." And the situation is, if anything, worse today. Not only are we in a terrible rush to "succeed," to reach a certain level of material and financial prosperity which we erroneously believe will lead to our well-being and happiness, but we are also barraged from all sides with all manner of information, some of which is useful and entertaining, but much of which is wholly irrelevant to our higher needs and pursuits, to our growth and fulfillment in life. We are surrounded with the constant noise and stimulus of television, radio, newspapers, and magazines. Countless advertisements, written, spoken, and visual, appeal to our baser needs and urge us to buy all kinds of unnecessary products and services, to follow the latest trend, and to dress, act, and look a certain way so that we may enjoy the envy of those around us. Our mental diet is, to a large degree, void of nutrients; we subsist on the intellectual equivalent of fats and sugars and suffer from the stunted growth, from the anxiety, depression, and mental lethargy, that inevitably result from such imbalance.

It is difficult, and it requires continued discipline and determination, to maintain our sense of direction and integrity in a world that in so many ways, blatant and subtle, conspires against us. It is far easier to yield to laziness, to get comfortable and to stop caring. In "The Snows of Kilimanjaro," Ernest Hemingway tells the story of a man who sacrifices his talents as a writer to

Insist on yourself; never imitate. Your own gift you can present every moment with the cumulative force of a whole life's cultivation; but of the adopted talent of another you have only an extemporaneous half possession. That which each can do best, none but his Maker can teach him. . . . Where is the master who could have taught Shakespeare? Where is the master who could have instructed Franklin, or Washington, or Bacon, or Newton?

RALPH WALDO EMERSON

his all-too-human desire for comfort and ease. On a safari with his wealthy wife, he has contracted gangrene and lies dying on a hot and dusty African plain, just below beautiful, ice-capped Mt. Kilimanjaro. The disease has progressed so far that the nerves in his infected leg have been killed; although there is no pain, there is a terrible smell, and hideous vultures have circled and begun landing nearby, waiting. The man knows that death is imminent.

Lying on his cot, he thinks back on all the stories he had planned to write, that had been his duty to write, but which he never completed. Instead he had saved them "until he knew enough to write them well." His considerable talents had helped him enter the society of the very rich (where he met his present wife, his "caretaker"), and for the past several years he has languished in pleasure and comfort. Rather than utilizing his talents, he traded on them; rather than what he was doing, it was always what he could do. This slowly drained his passion and desire. "Each day of not writing, of comfort," writes Hemingway, "of being that which he despised, dulled his ability and softened his will to work so that, finally, he did no work at all." Now he would not have another chance. The man's death is physically painless, but like that of Ivan Ilyich in Tolstoy's story, it is spiritually agonizing as he looks back at his squandered talents and ideals, at his wasted life.

All of us who wish to do something with our lives must come to terms with our natural inclination for ease and comfort, with our natural reluctance to move for-

*Security is mostly a superstition. It
does not exist in nature. . . . Life is either
a daring adventure or nothing.*

HELEN KELLER

*One can choose to go back toward safety
or forward toward growth. Growth must
be chosen again and again; fear must
be overcome again and again.*

ABRAHAM MASLOW

ward and to make a commitment. "There are risks and costs to a program of action," said John F. Kennedy in a statement that is as valid spiritually and psychologically as it is politically; "but they are far less than the long-range risks and costs of comfortable inaction." Staying where we are, waiting for just the right moment to act on our dreams, can give us a false feeling of power and potential. Rather than writing our book, painting our picture, or pursuing our ideal, we can keep it a possibility and smugly feel that it will be done, perhaps tomorrow or next week; we can harbor the comforting illusion that we can be someone special without the pain and risks that would accompany decision and action. Like the writer in Hemingway's story, we trade on what we can do rather than on what we are doing or have done. But there is a price for this inaction; for at a deeper level, at the core of our being which somehow knows the truth, we sense that we are deceiving ourselves, and that, to be whole, we must have courage and take action. With each passing day, however, our resolve weakens, and we become progressively incapable of initiative and work. "Iron rusts from disuse," wrote Leonardo da Vinci in his journals; "water loses its purity from stagnation and in cold weather becomes frozen; even so does inaction sap the vigors of the mind."

It is a common thing to like the feeling of power that comes with having many choices. As a young adult, for example, we may fancy becoming a doctor, a lawyer, an artist, an entrepreneur, a world traveler, or any of a dozen other alternatives. Rather than choose, which we

*There is always hope in a man that
actually and earnestly works: in
idleness alone is there perpetual despair.*
THOMAS CARLYLE

*Shun idleness. It is a rust that attaches
itself to the most brilliant metals.*
VOLTAIRE

The hardest work is to go idle.
JEWISH PROVERB

feel would be limiting, we may prefer to keep our options open, to be full of promise and potential. While it is certainly important to reflect and consider our alternatives before making a decision that will effect the course of our lives, this lack of decision can, at a certain point, become ridiculous and demoralizing. We may in time come to realize that to have a lot of possibilities means to have no possibility, that freedom actually comes from making a choice, from liberating ourselves from inaction and petty distractions so that we may follow the path that will lead to our greatest growth and satisfaction.

We may furthermore realize that ease and comfort, while an important part of our lives, can also be a hindrance to our growth and fulfillment. "The Superior Man cherishes excellence," said Confucius; "the Inferior Man, his own comfort." Confucius and a number of other philosophers were perhaps too intolerant of our natural inclination for comfort. Life is difficult, and we all need periods of rest, a refuge of simple pleasures which helps restore our energy and enthusiasm. "What is without periods of rest will not endure," said Ovid. What is more, it seems wrong that we get so caught up in our work, in our desire to grow and to fulfill our capabilities, that we, like Darwin, lose our ability to enjoy the natural treasures of life. Seizing the moment to enjoy life is a talent in itself that we must also develop and express. Like other talents, it will slowly atrophy and disappear if we do not nurture it and make it grow. "The great man is he who does not lose his child's

Shared joy is double joy,
and shared sorrow is half-sorrow.

SWEDISH PROVERB

If I had my life to live over again, I
would have made a rule to read some
poetry and listen to some music at least
once a week; for perhaps the parts of
my brain now atrophied would have
thus been kept active through use. The
loss of these tastes is a loss of happiness,
and may possibly be injurious to the
intellect, and more probably to the
moral character, by enfeebling the
emotional part of our nature.

CHARLES DARWIN

heart," said the Chinese philosopher Mencius. "There is more to life than increasing its speed," said Mahatma Gandhi. "Man will hereafter be called to account for depriving himself of the good things which the world lawfully allows," says the Talmud.

Yet, paradoxically, if our desire for comfort and pleasure becomes our dominant motive, determining the decisions we make and the path we follow, then it may actually defeat itself. For if we seek comfort to the exclusion of the fulfillment of our potential, pleasure rather than a meaningful and worthwhile pursuit, rest rather than life, then there will be an emptiness or an anxiety inside that will prevent us from knowing the higher satisfactions of existence, and perhaps even from truly partaking in its simple joys. "A man is relieved and gay when he has put his heart into his work and done his best," wrote Ralph Waldo Emerson; "what he has said or done otherwise shall give him no peace." The key, as with almost all other issues in life, lies in balance, in finding a middle way.

Likewise, if we seek security rather than the realization of our abilities, safety rather than growth, then we will be accentuating and developing our capacity for fear rather than courage, and security will, paradoxically, always remain slightly outside of our reach. Life, to be sure, is difficult and fraught with uncertainty. Socially, politically, and economically, we live in a perilous age; we sense that the earth may give way beneath our feet and that we will tumble down a bluff and into a sea of turmoil where we will scarcely be able to manage the

*People in the West are always
getting ready to live.*
CHINESE PROVERB

*A greater poverty than that caused by
lack of money is the poverty of
unawareness. Men and women go about
the world unaware of the beauty, the
goodness, the glories in it. Their souls
are poor. It is better to have a poor
pocketbook than to suffer from a poor soul.*
THOMAS DREIER

Money often costs too much.
RALPH WALDO EMERSON

strong currents and keep our head above the cold, dark swells. Even with regard to our personal lives, we recognize that there are many things beyond our control, that there are no guarantees that our efforts will yield the results that we desire. Thus we seek to build a refuge of security in which we can safely reside. There is no doubt that this, to a degree, is important, especially if we have a family to provide for and protect. But the thicker the walls we build to protect ourselves from life, the thicker the walls that may also prevent us from living; in securing ourselves against the winds of fortune, we may also be tying ourselves down and making it difficult or impossible to move forward toward growth and maturity.

It is therefore important that we find the courage to live our lives fully, to develop our talents and to give the world what Emerson called the only true gift, a portion of ourselves. "One does not discover new lands without consenting to lose sight of the shore for a very long time," wrote André Gide. Indeed, we must be willing to take risks, to leave the safe and familiar, if we are to explore our capacities and become what we are capable of becoming. While we should be careful not to put ourselves or our loved ones in unnecessary jeopardy, while our decisions and pursuits should always be in accordance with our means and capabilities, while our voyage across the sea of life should be well planned, using the best instruments of navigation at our disposal, stocking our vessel with the necessary provisions for our well-being and survival, we still must be willing to leave port

The highest insight a man can attain is the yearning for peace, for the union of his will with an infinite will, his human will with God's will. Such a will does not cut itself off and live in isolation like a puddle that is bound to dry up when the heat of the summer comes. No, it is like a mountain stream, relentlessly splashing its way to the river, there to be swept on to the limitless ocean.

ALBERT SCHWEITZER

and to set sail over unknown waters for the destination of our greatest talents, for the shore of our dearest dreams. There is no doubt that there will be times when the passage is difficult, when we are stranded in the doldrums or violently tossed by strong winds and ominous seas, but this is the price we must pay for growth and fulfillment. Our alternative is to hide from life, to deprive the world of our gift, and to live in a bleak existence that knows neither great suffering nor great joy.

III

SEIZE

THE DAY

———

Dostoevski, in his novel *The Idiot*, tells the story of a man who has been sentenced to death. He is led to the scaffold where he is to be executed and a priest comes to him with the cross. He has only five more minutes to live. But then, just before the sentence is to be carried out, he is given a reprieve and condemned to another punishment instead. These five minutes, when he thinks that death is imminent, seemed to him "like an infinite time, a vast wealth," he said. But "nothing was so dreadful at the time as the continual thought, 'What if I were not to die! What if I could go back to life—what eternity! And it would all be mine! I would turn every minute into an age; I would lose nothing, I would count every minute as it passed, I would not waste one!' He said that this idea turned to such a fury at last that he longed to be shot quickly."

This passage, which is based on Dostoevski's own

Short as life is, we make it still shorter
by the careless waste of time.
VICTOR HUGO

Dost thou love life? Then do not
squander time, for that is the
stuff life is made of.
BENJAMIN FRANKLIN

It is the wisest who grieve most
at the loss of time.
DANTE

reprieve after he had been sentenced to be executed by a firing squad, affirms the supreme value of life in the face of death. It is easy for us to get lost in a world of trivial urgencies and petty concerns, to let the minutes and hours of our lives go by without a thought for their irretrievability and worth. In fact, sometimes the demands of the day and the unspoken pressures of our age can be so overbearing that we feel quite unhappy and maybe even despise our lives. But if you were sentenced to death, if you had only a few more minutes or hours or days to live, how then would you feel about your life? And what, in retrospect, would you wish you could do differently? Your answer to these questions should determine the path that you follow, the way in which you presently live.

In truth, we are all sentenced to die, and whether we part from this miraculous existence in five minutes or five years or fifty, our time is brief and should be guarded and used with great love and care. "The hour which gives us life begins to take it away," said Seneca. "Like as waves make toward the pebbled shore, so do our minutes hasten to their end," wrote Shakespeare. Death limits our existence, but it also helps give it meaning; for if we had an eternity on this planet to work out our problems, to realize our talents and potentials, then there would be no urgency or reason to act now rather than later, and our days and weeks would be stripped of much of their purpose and value.

It has been suggested that in moments of deepest concentration, we regard our lives, and those who are a

You waste the treasure of your time.
WILLIAM SHAKESPEARE

The future is purchased by the present.
SAMUEL JOHNSON

*By the street of By-and-By, one
arrives at the house of Never.*
MIGUEL DE CERVANTES

part of our lives, as though we have already lost them to death, only to retrieve them back for a little while. This, in effect, is the experience of Dostoevski's prisoner, and such reflection makes us profoundly aware of the value of the passing minutes and hours of our existence, as well as of the value of our family and friends and the importance of their respective happiness and well-being. We do not have an eternity to work out our problems, to realize our potential, and to live our lives fully. We must begin now, or our resolve weakens, our energy diminishes, and doing so becomes increasingly difficult and unlikely. Our lives are the sum of the passing hours and days which we often so carelessly throw away. We are prone to kill time when we should strive to make it live.

Each of us has a unique contribution to make to the world, to life. Never before has a person been born with precisely your characteristics, with your blend of experiences, values, and talents. Never before has anyone had your distinct vision of a better world. These differences, the things that make each person unique, are also what make each indispensable and irreplaceable. Only you can fulfill your destiny and make your vision a reality.

It is impossible to tell a person what path he should follow, and those who would do so, who would try to influence and control the lives of their children or others beyond sympathetic encouragement and loving support, are doing them a disservice. Only you, in stillness and humility, can listen to the dictates of the still small

*I respect the man who knows distinctly
what he wishes. The greater part of
all the mischief in the world arises from
the fact that men do not sufficiently
understand their own aims. They have
undertaken to build a tower, and spend
no more labor on the foundation than
would be necessary to erect a hut.*

JOHANN WOLFGANG VON GOETHE

*He who would arrive at the appointed
end must follow a single road and
not wander through many ways.*

SENECA

voice which guides you—not perhaps all at once, but slowly, tenderly—to your most satisfying path. Only you can sense what direction your life must take in order to fulfill your highest destiny, and only you can find the will and discipline to follow this path with all your strength and all your heart.

It is encouraging to think that we are almost always free to start again. Regardless of what wrong turn we might have taken, we can, from this day, resolve to live the life we have glimpsed in moments of blessed inspiration, developing our special talents, enjoying the wonders of existence, making our life a gift to the world. Regardless of the mistakes we have made, the people we have hurt, the opportunities we have squandered, the time we have wasted, we can, from this moment, decide to make the most of the remaining days and years which we have been given to enjoy and to live. "From the lowest depth there is a path to the loftiest height," wrote Carlyle.

To do so, however, requires that we focus on what is important—on what takes us closer to our goals, on what enables us to live our lives most fully—and to refrain, insofar as possible, from what is not important. Our days have become terribly busy and complicated. We live in a hurried age, full of restlessness, noise, and activity. Much of what we do leads us nowhere and consumes the substance of our life like a slow-burning fire. Rushing this way and that, taking care of the many demands and urgencies that press upon us, we exhaust our energies and are dismayed to see that little of worth

It is not enough to be busy; so are the
ants. The question is: What are
we busy about?

HENRY DAVID THOREAU

One day Alice came to a fork in the
road and saw a Cheshire cat in a tree.
"Which road do I take?" she asked.
His response was a question:
"Where do you want to go?"
"I don't know," Alice answered.
"Then," said the cat,
"it doesn't matter."

LEWIS CARROLL

actually gets accomplished. "Paralyzed by a thousand and one considerations, we never get to the point of allowing free play to whatever greatness may be burgeoning within us," said Goethe.

A great deal of what we do can be replaced, if we choose, by activities that exercise our greater talents and abilities, that take us closer to our dreams. It is a matter of being conscious of our time and using it effectively. We may ask ourselves, at moments throughout the day, "Is what I am doing or about to do truly important? Does it express my greatest talents, does it take me closer to my most cherished ideals? Is it the best contribution I can make to my job, my family, to the world in which I live, at this time?" If the answer is no, and if we have the freedom to do the greater thing, then we must seize the moment and do so. "Our lives are frittered away by detail," said Thoreau, counseling that we strive for "simplicity and elevation of purpose." And La Rochefoucauld warned, "Those who give too much attention to trifling things become generally incapable of great ones."

The great thing that we decide to pursue will become the distant star by which we navigate our life. Perhaps we are called to grow and blossom where we have been sown, to honor our commitments and responsibilities by doing better and more conscientious work in the place of our employment, by being a more loving and empathic parent, child, or spouse. Perhaps we have a special dream or talent that must be developed and pursued if we are to fulfill our highest destiny. Only

Greatness of soul consists not so much in soaring high and in pressing forward, as in knowing how to adapt and limit oneself.
MICHEL DE MONTAIGNE

In all things, success depends upon previous preparation, and without such preparation there is sure to be failure.
CONFUCIUS

A field, however fertile, cannot be fruitful without cultivation, neither can a mind without learning.
CICERO

you can determine your path, and it is your foremost challenge to do so. Then you must do what you can to simplify your life so that you can direct as much precious time and energy as possible to your goal. "As a gardener, by severe pruning, forces the sap of the tree into one or two vigorous limbs, so should you stop off your miscellaneous activity and concentrate your force on one or a few points," advised Emerson.

Although your strength lies in originality, although your purpose must come from the depths of your being, there is much that you can learn from those who have come before you. Over two centuries ago, the artist Sir Joshua Reynolds gave a series of lectures at Oxford University on the nature of creativity and the development of the artist. While stressing the importance of originality, he said that the daily food and nourishment of the artist should be the great works of his predecessors. In studying and contemplating these works of genius, the artist is warmed by their contact and captures their spirit of excellence and simplicity. Furthermore, he combines what he has learned from studying these masterpieces with his own experience of nature and life and comes up with new forms and patterns. "Invention, strictly speaking," said Reynolds, "is little more than a new combination of those images which have been previously gathered and deposited in memory. Nothing can be made of nothing; he who has laid up no materials can produce no combinations."

Many of the most inventive and ingenious figures of the ages have acknowledged the importance of edu-

*Do not worry about holding a high
position; worry rather about playing
your proper role. Worry not that no one
knows you; seek to be worth knowing.*

CONFUCIUS

*Our grand business is not to see what
lies dimly at a distance, but to do
what lies clearly at hand.*

THOMAS CARLYLE

*To improve the golden moment of
opportunity, and catch the good that is
within our reach, is the great art of life.*

SAMUEL JOHNSON

cation, of preparation, and the debt they felt to those who came before them. "If I have seen further it is by standing on the shoulders of giants," said Isaac Newton. "The roots of education are bitter, but its fruit is sweet," commented Aristotle. Albert Einstein acknowledged, "Many times a day I realize how much my own outer and inner life is built upon the labors of my fellow men, both living and dead, and how earnestly I must exert myself in order to give in return as much as I have received." And Louis Pasteur noted, "In the field of observation, chance favors the prepared mind."

Preparation is indispensable to progress. Regardless of the way we choose, we can learn from others who have also turned their backs on mediocrity and conformity and set forth for the glorious peaks of their highest abilities and aspirations. Although their path will be necessarily different from ours, we can draw strength and encouragement from their example and learn from their achievements and mistakes. In many cases, they have charted maps and chronicled the difficulties that we may encounter on our journey; they have climbed to the heights of their respective destiny and described for us what they have seen. At a certain point, however, their experience and advice will no longer be able to help us. We will pass them on our journey or we will have to turn and follow a different route, a distinct approach to our personal summit.

Your journey to the summit of your talents begins where you are, with a single step. "Small opportunities are often the beginning of great enterprises," said De-

Whatever you do or dream you can do—begin it. Boldness has genius and power and magic in it.

JOHANN WOLFGANG VON GOETHE

Action is eloquence.

WILLIAM SHAKESPEARE

A man must make his opportunity as oft as find it.

FRANCIS BACON

mosthenes. "From a little spark may burst a mighty flame," said Dante. Often we are reluctant to take this first step because we do not feel prepared; we want everything to be just right before we get started. But the truth is, things will never be just right, since we can always have relatively more time, energy, money, and knowledge before beginning. The question, therefore, is not what we would do if we had better means, but what we will do with the means which we have; not what we would do if we had better opportunities, but what we will do with the opportunities at hand. "Try to put well in practice what you already know," advised the artist Rembrandt; "and in so doing, you will, in good time, discover the hidden things you now inquire about."

Perhaps we do not like the idea of starting at the bottom; we would prefer that something or someone lift us directly to the top. This might occasionally happen, but more often than not, the hand that will help us is at the end of our own sleeve, and those who are lifted to the top miss a splendid journey and suffer from altitude sickness. It is important that we resolve to be our own helper and not rely solely on others for support. Rather than waiting for something favorable to turn up, for someone to give us a boost, we must decide to uncover our own opportunities, or to create them even when none exist.

The place to begin, the thing that will lead us upward, is often right before us; it is a simple and common task, perhaps part of the responsibilities of our day. It

One of these days is none of these days.
ENGLISH PROVERB

*What may be done at any time will
be done at no time.*
SCOTTISH PROVERB

*Things do not happen. They are
made to happen.*
JOHN F. KENNEDY

may not be a giant leap, but it is a step, and if we do it well, to the best of our ability, it will lead us upward to the next step, and to the next. "Our grand business is not to see what lies dimly at a distance, but to do what lies clearly at hand," advised Thomas Carlyle. "Human felicity is produced, not so much by great pieces of good fortune that seldom happen, as by little advantages that occur every day," observed Benjamin Franklin. "Practice yourself, for heaven's sake, in little things; and thence proceed to greater," said Epictetus. "Slight not what's near through aiming at what's far," wrote Euripides. "The only way to begin on top," says the proverb, "is to dig a hole."

In realizing that we must make our opportunity rather than wait for it, we are humbled by a grave yet exhilarating sense of responsibility for our existence. Even though there are many things that lie outside our sphere of influence and control, we, to a significant degree, shape our lives by the decisions we make, by the actions we take. At any given moment, on any given day, there are a multitude of things that we can choose to do. One of these things we decide upon and make a permanent part of our lives and a permanent part of the world in which we live. In this way, we shape and are responsible for our own destiny, as well as for the destiny of mankind. In this lies our greatest freedom, our most awesome responsibility.

Often we are afraid to take the first step. We sense that there will be heartache and pain on the road ahead; we fear that our dreams will be shattered, that we will

*It is a rough road that leads to
the heights of greatness.*

SENECA

*The greater the difficulty, the more
glory in surmounting it. Skillful
pilots gain their reputation from
storms and tempests.*

EPICURUS

*The gem cannot be polished
without friction, nor man
perfected without trials.*

CHINESE PROVERB

stumble and look foolish. This is not without good reason. Life is difficult; there will certainly be troubles on the road ahead; there will certainly be pain as we test our ideals against reality, as we try to find our way. But in acting, in taking our first step, and then the next, we arrive at the higher realization that life is not only conflict and tribulation, but that it can also be victory, transcendence, and growth. In acting, in being willing to endure pain in order to experience joy, we open our eyes and see the splendid colors and textures of life; we open our ears and hear its beautiful harmonies and rhythms; we taste its bitterness, but we also experience its sweetness.

The moments of our lives are irreplaceable and invaluable. Each opportunity to add to the quality of our existence, to choose growth and the expression of our talents, is taken or lost forever. It is how we seize the day, how we make use of our time, that ultimately determines the quality and direction of our life. Today is the necessary product of our yesterdays; our tomorrows are shaped by how we live today. We must therefore find the courage to take the first step, and then the next, so that we can make our way to our highest destiny. In so doing we will have given ourselves momentum, however slight, and we will have turned our backs on mediocrity and conformity to face the radiant white peaks of our greatest potential. We will already begin to feel the cool, fresh mountain air in our face and to sense the richness of the soil beneath our feet.

But what if something holds us back, something

*There is no situation that cannot be
ennobled by achievement or enduring.*
JOHANN WOLFGANG VON GOETHE

*Every noble crown is, and on earth
will ever be, a crown of thorns.*
THOMAS CARLYLE

*One must learn to endure what
cannot be escaped.*
MICHEL DE MONTAIGNE

that is beyond our control—a debilitating illness, for example, or a cruel and oppressive environment from which we cannot possibly get free? We have already seen how difficult it is to move forward in life if we are suffering through a personal crisis or a loss of confidence and faith. The best we can do, at times like these, is to cope with the demands of daily living, to gradually learn the lessons of our suffering, and to heal, to become whole again. But what if our crisis is so severe, so harsh, that healing and freedom are impossible? What if that which holds us back is something we cannot change, regardless of our strength, determination, and patience— something we can only endure?

Viktor Frankl has written at length about his nightmarish experiences in the Nazi death camps. At Auschwitz, he faced horrors which words cannot adequately describe: hunger, cold, lack of sleep, exhausting work, physical and mental torture, the constant threat of death. Yet even under these hellish conditions, men and women were able to give their lives meaning, says Frankl; they were able to choose the way in which they endured their suffering. "We who lived in the concentration camps can remember the men who walked through the huts comforting others, giving away their last piece of bread. They may have been few in number, but they offer sufficient proof that everything can be taken away from a man but one thing: this last of human freedoms—to choose one's attitude in any given set of circumstances, to choose one's own way."

Sigmund Freud believed that if a group of men

*We must never forget that we may also
find meaning in life even when confronted
with a hopeless situation, when facing
a fate that cannot be changed. For what
then matters is to bear witness to the
uniquely human potential at its best,
which is to transform a personal tragedy
into a triumph, to turn one's predicament
into a human achievement. When we are
no longer able to change a situation—
just think of an incurable disease such as
inoperable cancer—we are challenged
to change ourselves.*

VIKTOR FRANKL

faced starvation, all of their individual differences would disappear and they would be motivated solely by their need to survive. Thank heaven Freud was not a prisoner in the concentration camps, says Frankl; but if he had been, he would have seen that this is not true. Even under the worst of conditions, even facing death and withstanding man's inhumanity to man, individuals can choose how they respond; and they do, in fact, respond differently. Dostoevski wrote, "There is only one thing that I dread: not to be worthy of my sufferings." These words came frequently to Frankl's mind as he got to know those men whose "behavior in camp, whose suffering and death, bore witness to the fact that the last inner freedom cannot be lost. It can be said that they were worthy of their sufferings; the way they bore their suffering was a genuine inner achievement. It is this spiritual freedom—which cannot be taken away—that makes life meaningful and purposeful." Even under unspeakably horrible and unfair conditions, therefore, we can find purpose; we can still strive to fulfill values which give our lives meaning; we can still decide what kind of person we become.

Most of us, thankfully, are not prisoners or victims of such cruel or harsh circumstances. We are relatively free to pursue our dreams and to find creative work which makes use of our talents and abilities. The way we choose to do this work, nevertheless, also has a profound effect on the person we become. Carl Jung once wrote that the work of the poet determines his psychic development: "It is not Goethe who creates *Faust*, but

*Everything that happens to us leaves
some trace behind: everything
contributes imperceptibly to
make us what we are.*

JOHANN WOLFGANG VON GOETHE

*It does not matter so much what you
do, what matters is whether your soul is
harmed by what you do. If your soul is
harmed, something irreparable happens,
the extent of which you won't realize
until it will be too late.*

ALBERT SCHWEITZER

Faust which creates Goethe." This is true of all work and regardless of what we do, regardless of what talents we express, we should recognize that the way in which we carry out the tasks before us is reflected back in our spirit and character. We create our work, our work creates us. "Their works do follow them," says the Bible. "What you are is the sum of everything you have said and done," said the Buddha. "Our characters are the result of our conduct," commented Aristotle. "Our acts make or mar us—we are the children of our own deeds," wrote Victor Hugo.

Unfortunately, many of us are more concerned with external measures of success than with personal integrity. Often we measure our progress and worth by how much money we make and by how many fine possessions adorn our lives; sometimes, like Tolstoy's Ivan Ilyich, we are willing to sacrifice our values, our sense of truth and compassion, in order to achieve these ends. But what does any of this mean if our souls are empty or corrupt? Of what worth are external riches if we suffer from internal poverty? Wherever we go, our character goes with us; however we dress, we cannot hide our soul. "If we have not quiet in our minds," wrote Bunyan, "outward comfort will do no more good for us than a golden slipper on a gouty foot."

Regardless of where we are, regardless of what we do, the tasks and responsibilities before us, the challenges of the day, are of vital importance to our growth and sense of integrity. At the core of our being, we somehow know the truth about ourselves, and we suffer

*Do what you reprove yourself for
not doing. Know that you are neither
satisfied nor dissatisfied with
yourself without reason.*

HENRY DAVID THOREAU

*All is well with you even though
everything seems to go dead wrong, if you
are square with yourself. Reversely,
all is not well with you, although
everything outwardly may seem to go
right, if you are not square with yourself.*

MAHATMA GANDHI

when we do things superficially, when we do less than we are paid for (a form of stealing) or less than we can expect of ourselves. Each slighted responsibility, each poorly performed task, chips away at our sense of worth and self-respect. We lose faith in ourselves and in our own goodness.

Doing our best, however, working with love, giving rather than taking, makes us feel whole; kindness, generosity, and compassion are reflected in our spirit rather than egoism and dishonesty. For this reason, if we do not feel compelled to give our best, if we are not presently trying to express our highest talents and abilities, then it would perhaps be better to change positions, to get in a place that calls out our deeper affections. "It is not what we do but how much love we put into it," says Mother Teresa. "Work is love made visible," writes Gibran. "And if you cannot work with love but only with distaste, it is better that you should leave your work and sit at the gate of the temple and take alms of those who work with joy. For if you bake bread with indifference, you bake a bitter bread that feeds but half a man's hunger. And if you grudge the crushing of the grapes, your grudge distills a poison into the wine."

Nothing of value can be accomplished in this world without love, hard work, and sacrifice. The greater your dream, the more you expect of yourself, the more you are called by God to do, the more discipline and strength it will take you to reach your goals. "Long is the road from conception to completion," said Molière. "Those who aim at great deeds must also suffer greatly," ob-

Accustom yourself to complete any good work you have undertaken.
THE TALMUD

Diligence is the mother of good fortune.
MIGUEL DE CERVANTES

A man without determination is but an untempered sword.
CHINESE PROVERB

served Plutarch. Unfortunately, however, we live in an age when people expect things to happen instantly; in fact, it is considered a virtue if we can do things easily and get immediate results, if we can become an "overnight success." In a sense, we have lost touch with the rhythm of the earth, with the march of the seasons. We mistakenly expect to throw some seeds on the ground and to have them yield an immediate and abundant harvest. We forget that the fields must be carefully tilled and cultivated; that the seeds we sow must be nourished and cared for with the water of hope and the sunlight of love and faith; that we must have the patience to wait for them to grow, blossom, and come to fruition. "The greatest secret of life is to know how to wait," said de Maistre.

Part of the problem stems perhaps from the publicity and homage paid to sweepstakes winners and those who get rich quickly (in some cases their stories would be better reported on the obituary page). Another factor could be that we live at a time in which commerce and technology are largely concerned with doing things easier and faster. Many of us have come to embody this appetite for expediency and convenience; rather than focusing on the development and expression of our talents and on the results we wish to achieve, we concentrate on finding easy and pleasing methods. The results do not matter so long as we can get by without too much effort. This is a mistake. In observing those who fulfill their talents and abilities, who realize their ideals, we see that they look beyond comfortable and pleasing meth-

How poor are they that have not patience!
WILLIAM SHAKESPEARE

Patience is bitter, but its fruit is sweet.
JEAN-JACQUES ROUSSEAU

Have patience and the mulberry leaf will become satin.
SPANISH PROVERB

ods and focus on that which they wish to achieve. They willingly give up a safe and easy path and instead focus on the distant peaks of their highest dreams and aspirations. Then, with patience and determination, they find or forge a trail to get there.

It has been said that genius is the infinite capacity for taking pains, and many of the most creative spirits who have walked this earth would humbly agree. "If I have done the public any service," commented Sir Isaac Newton, "it is due to patient thought." "Let me tell you the secret that has led me to my goal," said Louis Pasteur; "my strength lies solely in my tenacity." Albert Einstein observed, "I think and think for months and years. Ninety-nine times, the conclusion is false. The hundredth time I am right." And Sigmund Freud wrote, "From error to error one discovers the whole truth."

In the arts, too, excellence is achieved through hard work, patience, and persistence. "God sells us all things at the price of labor," said Leonardo da Vinci. "The best of me is diligence," wrote Shakespeare. "Work is my chief pleasure," said Mozart. Charles Dickens commented, "My own invention or imagination, such as it is, I can most truthfully assure you, would never have served me as it has but for the commonplace, humble, patient, daily, toiling, drudging attention." And Montesquieu, speaking of one of his writings, said, "You will read it in a few hours, but I assure you that it has cost me so much labor that it has whitened my hair."

In pursuing our dreams, in developing our talents, it is inevitable that we will run up against obstacles that

What on earth would a man do with himself if something did not stand in his way?

H. G. WELLS

Lord, grant that I may always desire more than I can accomplish.

MICHELANGELO

Life is occupied both in perpetuating itself and in surpassing itself; if all it does is maintain itself, then living is only not dying, and human existence is indistinguishable from an absurd vegetation.

SIMONE DE BEAUVOIR

will try our faith and test the limits of our endurance. At times, as we climb to our personal summit, we look ahead and it appears that our path is blocked and that further progress will be impossible; dismayed, we believe that we have traveled far and suffered much for naught. But if we have courage and continue, we get closer and see that the path is not actually blocked, but that it stretches gently around a corner and continues on to our goal. "I find nothing so singular in life as this," said Hawthorne, "that everything opposing appears to lose its substance the moment one actually grapples with it."

At other times, however, our path does, indeed, lead to a dead end or is blocked by some obstruction that seems insurmountable. These are the moments that test our will and determination, that call out the strength of our spirit. Sometimes we can chisel away at the boulder that blocks our path, finding a way over or around it. At other times, however, we have to temporarily retreat, taking a few steps back to reflect on the merits of our pursuit and on whether we should, in fact, continue (no sense throwing good efforts after a bad cause). If we do decide to press on, then we must summon the strength to find or make another path that will lead to our goal.

There is a wonderful fable, told by Aesop and La Fontaine, about a lion and a gnat. "Get away, you wretched insect, you scum of the earth!" says the lion to the gnat, who is offended and immediately declares war. "Do you think that I'm impressed or frightened because they call you king?" challenges the gnat. "The

Life affords no higher pleasure than that of surmounting difficulties, passing from one step of success to another, forming new wishes, and seeing them gratified. He that labors in any great or laudable undertaking has his fatigues first supported by hope, and afterwards rewarded by joy.

SAMUEL JOHNSON

Perseverance is a great element of success. If you only knock long enough and loud enough at the gate, you are sure to wake up somebody.

HENRY WADSWORTH LONGFELLOW

ox is stronger than you and I can make him do my bidding at the slightest sting." So saying this, the gnat charges into battle, pouncing on the lion's back and driving him mad with irritation. The lion is enraged and all the creatures in the area hide. The little gnat torments the lion and stings him in a hundred places, first on the back, then on the snout, and finally up his nose. Despair! It is amusing to see that neither tooth nor claw are needed to wound the furious animal. In agony and disarray, the unfortunate lion tears at his own flesh and beats feebly at the air. Until, at last, exhausted by rage, he collapses, quite done in. The victorious gnat, beaming in glory, retires from the fight, as he entered it, blowing his own horn. But as he buzzes around everywhere, boasting of his victory, he runs into a spider's web. And that is the end of him.

Like the gnat, we, too, can triumph over giant obstacles and overwhelming circumstances by stinging in a hundred places, by dividing and conquering, by breaking them into manageable pieces and then tackling them one at a time. However, also like the gnat, in escaping a great danger we can often fall prey to a smaller one, especially when we are gloating over our previous triumphs. We must therefore always be attentive, cautious, and resolute.

Most of our achievements are preceded by failure. Our predicament is that we live in a society that is obsessed with the appearance of success. We place such a high value on looking successful, as if our lives are in order and that things could not be better, that we are

Only those who dare to fail greatly
can ever achieve greatly.
ROBERT KENNEDY

Our greatest glory is not in never
falling, but in rising every time we fall.
CONFUCIUS

Failure is the foundation of success,
and the means by which it is achieved.
Success is the lurking place of failure;
but who can tell when the turning
point will come?
LAO TSU

afraid to try anything that could make us look vulnerable and imperfect. We are desperately afraid of failing, and as a consequence, we hold ourselves back and make use of only a fraction of our abilities. The truth is, however, there is no such thing as final and absolute failure, just as there is no such thing as final and absolute success. Failure is nothing more than a response—albeit an often painful one; the world in which we act tells us that what we are doing is not what we must do to reach our goal. We need to make some adjustments in our approach or we need to try something new altogether. As a result, we are, in a sense, better off than we were before; we have learned that one approach does not work and we are free to try the next, with all the knowledge and experience gained from our first effort. Failure, therefore, is the way to success. Growth and the progressive realization of our talents and dreams are impossible without the pain of failure. A person who has never failed is a person who has never tested his limits.

And what if we could achieve our dreams and realize our talents without any pain, without any serious effort? Would there be much satisfaction? Or would we give little value to what comes too easy? The truth is, much of the satisfaction comes from the struggle, from the awareness and growth of our powers, from what we learn, from who we become in pursuit of our dreams. There is, to be sure, satisfaction in achieving our goals, but once we realize a certain level or plateau, it is not long before the healthy person is already looking beyond it to the next challenge.

It is provided in the essence of things that from any fruition of success, no matter what, shall come forth something to make a greater struggle necessary.

WALT WHITMAN

The road is always better than the inn.

MIGUEL DE CERVANTES

To travel, hopefully, is a better thing than to arrive, and the true success is to labor.

ROBERT LOUIS STEVENSON

There is the belief in our society that one actually attains "success," that one arrives at a certain point where work and growth are no longer necessary and where one can live blissfully off the rewards and satisfactions of his prior achievements. This belief is as dangerous as it is false. "Work is the inevitable condition of human life, the true source of human welfare," wrote Tolstoy. Indeed, if we are alive, if we can still draw breath and are reasonably aware of our talents and capabilities, then there is more that we can do, there is more we must do, if our lives are to go on having purpose and meaning, joy and satisfaction. "Life never ceases to put new questions to us," says Viktor Frankl. We are as young as our responsiveness to these questions, as old as our unwillingness to hear; we are as young as our faith, hope, and love, as old as our doubts, fears, and despair.

In the Parable of the Talents, the reward for work well done is more work. "You have shown that you are trustworthy in handling small things, so now I will trust you with greater," said the master to his worthy servants. He who has much, who finds and makes use of his talents, discovers that he has more to do. As he finds the courage to take action, so do his abilities grow; as his abilities grow, so do his dreams and aspirations. His life is full, rewarding, satisfying. But he who hides his talents, who succumbs to fear, laziness, and false values, forfeits even the little bit of satisfaction he once had. His life becomes stagnant, dark, and boring. It has progressively less purpose and satisfaction.

If I can stop one heart from breaking,
I shall not live in vain;
If I can ease one life the aching,
Or cool one pain,
Or help one fainting robin
Unto his nest again,
I shall not live in vain.

EMILY DICKINSON

Die when I may, I want it said of me
by those who knew me best, that I
always plucked a thistle and planted
a flower where I thought a
flower would grow.

ABRAHAM LINCOLN

It is in working, in developing our talents and pursuing our dreams, that we participate in life. There is so much that is wrong in the world, so much unnecessary pain, suffering, cruelty, and injustice. We know this, and where we know it, we can take steps to alleviate it. We have seen man at his best, in moments of beauty and compassion, taking steps to help his fellowman, to relieve suffering, to comfort the needy and afflicted, and to make the world a better and safer place. We have enjoyed the fruits of his labor, the beautiful music and art that took years of hard training to produce; the great literature and ideas that required a lifetime to discover and express; the many products and services that sustain us and that bring joy into our lives, thanks to the courage and hard work of the people who produce them. We have seen and experienced what is highest in human nature, and we know that a better world is possible.

The greatest danger in life lies in losing our sensitivity, our reverence for life and for the world in which we live. In our youth, we are often idealistic; we are full of passion for good and indignity for the injustices of the world. As we get older, however, we notice that the people around us have lost much of their compassion and sympathy. Sometimes the people who get the most attention and attain the most power seem to be cold and heartless to their fellowman. Maybe this is the way, we think, and we start to let our values slide. We decide that the world is indeed a hard place, and that the best we can do is protect ourselves, to get all we can, and not to worry about others.

Last night I thought in a dream that the shortest expression of the meaning of life is this: the world moves, is being perfected; it is man's task to contribute to this motion and to submit to and cooperate with it.

LEO TOLSTOY

A man, after he has brushed off the dust and chips of his life, will have left only the hard, clean question: was it good or was it evil? Have I done well—or ill?

JOHN STEINBECK

This is a dangerous path that leads away from the clear and spectacular mountaintops, past the concrete world of mere conformity, to a suffocating swamp from which it is difficult to get free. We can rationalize that we are animal in nature, that it is natural to compete, that the strong survive and prosper while the weak suffer and perish. In part this is true; nature is amoral, and we are part of nature. But what distinguishes humans, what makes us different from rodents and reptiles, is our consciousness of the value of life, our sympathy for other living things, our capacity for love, kindness, altruism. It is in fulfilling these characteristics that we live the life which is most distinctly human, which will lead to our fullest and most complete development and satisfaction.

Each of us, where he stands, can picture a better world and know his part in it. Whether it is being a good parent, friend, or employee, whether it is developing our special talents or pursuing our greatest dreams, there is something that each of us can do for that part of the world in which we live. The scope of what we do is not important. We have only to fulfill the tasks and responsibilities before us, to make use of our highest talents, to do the best we can, where we are, with what we have. "I know there are thousands and thousands of poor, but I think of only one at a time," said Mother Teresa. "A man has not everything to do, but something," counseled Thoreau.

In utilizing our talents, in serving God and our fellowman, we each have the opportunity to participate in life. This has been the lesson of many of the world's

Let us go forth to lead the land we love, asking His blessing and His help, but knowing that here on earth God's work must truly be our own.

JOHN F. KENNEDY

Human progress never rolls on the wheels of inevitability; it comes through the tireless efforts of men willing to be co-workers with God, and without this hard work, time itself becomes an ally of the forces of social stagnation. We must use time creatively, in the knowledge that the time is always ripe to do right

MARTIN LUTHER KING, JR.

great religions and philosophies. "Come and share in my happiness," said the master in the parable, to the servants who had the courage to use and multiply their talents and abilities. Perhaps God has given us each the chance to share in His happiness; perhaps we each have the opportunity to share in the joy, the exhilaration, the unparalleled fulfillment of participating in life, of creating the world in which we live.